SINGER

Sewing Activewear

Cy DeCosse Incorporated
Minnetonka, Minnesota

SINGER

SEWING REFERENCE LIBRARY®

Sewing Activewear

Contents

How to Use This Book 7

Copyright © 1986
Cy DeCosse Incorporated
5900 Green Oak Drive
Minnetonka, Minnesota 55343
1-800-328-3895
All rights reserved
Printed in U.S.A.

Also available from the publisher: *Sewing Essentials, Sewing for the Home, Clothing Care & Repair, Sewing for Style, Sewing Specialty Fabrics, The Perfect Fit, Timesaving Sewing, More Sewing for the Home, Tailoring, Sewing for Children, Sewing with an Overlock, 101 Sewing Secrets, Sewing Pants That Fit, Quilting by Machine*

Library of Congress
Cataloging-in-Publication Data

Sewing Activewear

(Singer Sewing Reference Library)
Includes index.
1. Sport clothes. I. Series
TT649.S47   1986   646'.47   85-29362
ISBN 0-86573-211-6
ISBN 0-86573-212-4 (pbk.)

Distributed by: Contemporary Books, Inc.
  Chicago, Illinois

CY DE COSSE INCORPORATED
Chairman: Cy DeCosse
President: James B. Maus
Executive Vice President: William B. Jones

SEWING ACTIVEWEAR
Created by: The Editors of Cy DeCosse Incorporated, in cooperation with the Singer Education Department. Singer is a trademark of the Singer Company and is used under license.

Managing Editor: Reneé Dignan
Project Director: Gail Devens

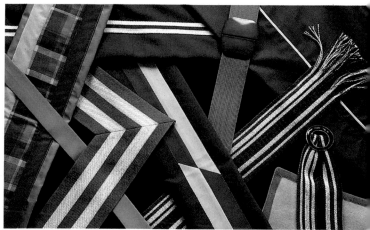

Senior Art Director: William Nelson
Art Director: Rebecca Gammelgaard
Writer: Peggy Bendel
Editors: Susan Meyers, Bernice Maehren
Sample Supervisor: Carol Neumann
Fabric Editor: Rita Opseth
Sewing Staff: Phyllis Galbraith, Bridget
  Haugh, Susan Bacheller, Kathleen Davis
  Ellingson, Wendy Fedie, Liz Hickerson,
  Jeanine Theroux
Photographers: Tony Kubat, John Lauenstein,
  Jerry Krause, Kris Boom, Jerry Robb
Production Manager: Jim Bindas
Assistant Production Manager: Julie Churchill

Production Staff: Michelle Alexander,
  Michelle Joy, Yelena Konrardy, Linda
  Schloegel, Cathy Shannon, Jennie Smith,
  Bryan Trandem, Nik Wogstad
Consultants: Zoe Graul, The Singer
  Company; Arleen Haislip, The Green
  Pepper, Inc.; JoAnn Krause; Judy Laube,
  Stretch & Sew; Teresa Wingert, Kwik-Sew
  Pattern Co., Inc.
Contributing Manufacturers: B. Blumenthal &
  Co., Inc.; Bow Ties Custom Racewear;
  Burlington Home Sewing Fabrics;
  Clotilde; Dan River; Dubens Sales
  Company; Dyno Merchandise Corporation;

Everitt Knitting Co.; EZ International;
The Green Pepper, Inc.; Guilford Mills,
Inc.; Hobbs Bonded Fibers; Kwik-Sew
Pattern Co., Inc.; Minnetonka Mills, Inc.;
Nancy's Notions; Polar Fleece® by Big
Apple Textiles; Rain Shed; Sew Easy
Industries; Stacy Fabric Corporation;
Streamline Industries, Inc.; Stretch &
Sew; Sunrise Industries, Inc.; Swiss-
Metrosene, Inc.; Thinsulate® by 3M;
Wrights Home Sewing Company; YKK
Home Sewing Division; YLI Corporation

Color Separations: La Cromolito
Printing: R. R. Donnelley & Sons Co. (0890)

How to Use This Book

Whether you are seriously involved in sports or just enjoy wearing sportswear fashions, *Sewing Activewear* shows you how to sew a wide selection of sportswear items. Use the information in this book to create items ranging from universally popular sweatsuits and warm-ups to specialized biking outfits and insulated outerwear.

Sewing your own sportswear offers a number of advantages. First, you can make simple pattern adjustments so the finished garment fits more attractively and comfortably than garments that are mass produced. Then, if you are making garments for specific sports or climate conditions, you can select exactly the fabrics you need for optimum performance. You can also choose attractive color combinations and add details and special trims for a custom-made look. As a final reward, making your own sportswear often costs considerably less than buying similar items.

A Guide to Fabrics & Supplies

Sportswear sewing is different from tailoring or fine dressmaking. One distinguishing factor is the use of fabrics such as thin insulations, two-way stretch knits, and shiny nylons woven so tightly that they repel water. The beginning pages of this book introduce you to special sportswear fabrics, insulations, notions, and other supplies. Each item is shown in a color photograph to help you recognize it when you shop.

A Handbook of Sewing Techniques

The importance of machine techniques is another feature of sportswear sewing. Most sportswear garments can be made entirely by machine. Machine techniques are fast and easy — one reason that even beginners can enjoy success when sewing sportswear.

The alternative techniques in *Sewing Activewear* can be used with any commercial pattern. In most cases, alternatives are provided for a conventional straight stitch or zigzag machine or for a serger (overlock machine), enabling you to use your equipment to the best advantage. Use methods that make sports garments durable and that build in an extra measure of quality. That may mean adapting the pattern to suit your needs. You can easily change the waistline of sweatpants, for example, from a casing finish to

stitched-on elastic. Or you may want to add a self-storing hood to a lightweight jacket. To make the garment more useful, you may decide to add pockets.

Throughout the book, step-by-step color photos show how to apply these techniques to achieve professional-looking results. Contrasting thread is sometimes used in the photographs so you can see the sewing techniques clearly; except for decorative stitching, you will want to use matching thread for your own projects.

A Source of Project Ideas

A final hallmark of sportswear sewing is style. Some garments are styled to function for a particular sport. Others are designed for comfort and can be worn for sports activities or casualwear. The four main sections of this book present project ideas organized according to sportswear style.

The first section covers actionwear, which includes closely fitted garments made from two-way stretch knits. These are garments worn for swimming, dancing, biking, gymnastics, aerobics, and ice skating.

The second section presents sportswear styled for comfort. Made from knits and lightweight woven fabrics, these are multi-purpose garments that fit loosely. Items such as sweatshirts, sweatpants, pull-on shorts, and lightweight pullover tops can be worn for leisure, as well as active participation in a sport.

The third section shows how to make sportswear styled for warmth and protection. Outdoor activities such as hiking, camping, and backpacking require insulated jackets and vests, waterproof outer shells, and layered separates.

The fourth section takes a fashion approach to sportswear. Using the same patterns, fabrics, and sewing techniques required for active sportswear, you can sew a fashionable wardrobe suitable for all-occasion use. This section shows how to add the creative touches of applied stripes, fold-over braid, piping, and custom belts.

When you have finished sewing, you will find you have received great value for the time spent. The appeal of sportswear is universal, so this book will be helpful whatever your age, activity, figure type, or sewing ability.

Getting Started

Fabrics for Action

When a sport or activity requires a wide range of body motion, highly elastic knits offer a number of practical benefits. These fabrics stretch in both directions, crosswise and lengthwise, so they are called two-way or four-way stretch knits.

Spandex is a man-made elastic fiber that is blended with other natural or man-made fibers to give a knit garment added stretch and the ability to retain its shape. Garments made from such knits are flexible, comfortable, and nonrestricting. Fit can be skintight to reveal the body in motion and to minimize wind resistance. Two-way stretch knit garments are lightweight, easy to care for, and quick drying. Many solid colors, stripes, and prints are available for wardrobe variety and creative costumes. All of these qualities are important if you participate in dancing, gymnastics, running, skating, swimming, bicycle racing, aerobics, skiing, or similar activities.

Two-way stretch knits come in several fiber combinations, which have different performance characteristics and surface textures. Nylon/spandex knits have a distinctive shine and excellent shape retention. Originally used for swimwear, nylon/spandex knits are now also used for other strong, formfitting garments such as bicycle shorts, tights, and dancewear.

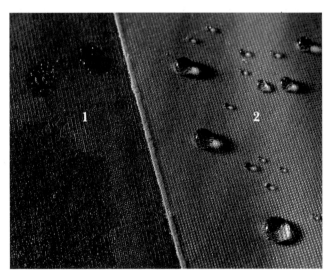

Absorbency. Cotton/polyester/spandex knits (1) have a matte surface and feel softer than nylon/spandex knits (2). They are more absorbent but do not dry as quickly and are slightly less durable. Although not as practical for swimwear, they can be used for many other sports, especially those enjoyed in hot weather, or for indoor workouts. Polypropylene/spandex knits do not absorb moisture, but allow it to escape through the fibers. For this reason, these knits offer good insulation. In cold weather they are useful for running tights, racing suits for skiing and cycling, and other garments worn next to the skin.

Fabrics for Comfort

Whether used for sport or leisure, garments such as sweatshirts, pull-on shorts or pants, and T-shirts are among the most versatile and comfortable items to sew. These loosely fitted styles can be layered over other garments or worn alone. When layered, they often serve as warm-ups over leotards or as cover-ups worn by the pool and on the way to the gym. They are worn alone for sailing, jogging, or leisure activities. Suitable fabrics include knits, wovens, and meshes.

Knits often used for these sportswear styles are sweatshirt fleece (**1**), velour (**2**), stretch terry (**3**), textured sweater knits (**4**), and double knits (**5**). Jersey (**6**) and interlock knits (**7**) are used for T-shirts and other pullover tops. Lightweight tricot (**8**) is often used for running shorts and sleeveless tank tops. Some of these knits have a one-direction stretch quality; others are stable and have little or no elasticity but get their comfort from loose, easy fit.

Woven fabrics recommended for casual garments include poplin (**9**), twill (**10**), and gabardine (**11**). Other sturdy mediumweight fabrics such as chino and plain weaves are also suitable.

Mesh knit fabrics (12), used as inserts, ventilate sportswear and provide an attractive contrast in texture. Various sizes of mesh are available in cotton, nylon, polyester, and blends.

As you select fabrics, notice the fiber content on the bolt-end label or hang tag. Fabrics made of all-cotton are likely to offer the most comfort because this fiber is absorbent and breathes. Follow care instructions closely because all-cotton fabrics may fade, shrink, and wrinkle unless special manufacturing finishes have been used.

Blends of cotton with polyester or acrylic fibers are easy to care for. They are more resistant to shrinkage and wrinkling than are fabrics made from pure cotton. These blends are less absorbent, which can be an advantage. The less moisture the fabric holds, the more quickly the garment dries when wet. But the higher the percentage of synthetic fiber, the less the fabric allows perspiration to evaporate.

Purely synthetic fabrics made from nylon, polyester, or acrylic fibers can be washed and dried by machine; they rarely require ironing. They are not absorbent, so they dry quickly. Colors are permanent; many of these fibers that tend to accumulate static electricity are treated to reduce static buildup.

Fabrics for Warmth & Protection

Outdoor activities such as hiking, cross-country skiing, camping, cycling, and running expose you to the climate and to sudden changes in weather. Select outerwear fabrics to provide efficient protection without adding undue weight or bulk. Some of these fabrics may be sold in local fabric stores; however, many are available through mail-order firms that make sports fabrics their specialty.

The following terms describe the practical benefits that outerwear fabrics can contribute to the sportswear you sew:

Breathable fabrics are porous to let perspiration evaporate, an important factor for comfort.

Easy-care fabrics can be machine washed and dried without ironing or other special pampering. Some fabrics dry quickly, a quality that outdoor sportspersons value.

Insulation proof, down proof, and fiber proof are equivalent terms describing a fabric that is so tightly woven that high-loft insulations, such as polyester fiberfill or down, will not pass through the weave. Fabrics without this quality can allow fibers to migrate through the weave to the outside of a garment; this is called *bearding*.

Strength is important; fragile fabrics will not withstand rugged outdoor abuse. A fabric may be strong because it is made from a durable fiber such as nylon, or its strength may come from a weave that is fine and tight.

Waterproof fabrics are coated or laminated so that moisture can neither enter nor penetrate the fabric. Although waterproof fabrics offer the ultimate protection from water, they are not breathable. Wearing comfort is sacrificed unless the garment is very loosely fitted or ventilated in some way.

Water repellent fabrics resist penetration by water. Water initially beads on the fabric surface but can pass through the fabric during prolonged exposure. Because water repellent fabrics are more porous than those that are waterproof, they are generally more breathable and more comfortable to wear.

Windproof fabrics will not allow air to pass through the fabric, either because of a chemical treatment applied during the manufacturing process or because the fabric has a fine, very tight weave.

Wind resistant fabrics keep much of the wind from passing through the weave. They are less efficient than windproof fabrics but may offer enough protection if you dress in layers.

Warm Fabrics

Quilted fabrics, or prequilts, are made with one or two outer fabric layers stitched to a puffy batting. When sewing outerwear, look for quilted fabrics with a nylon taffeta face. Those quilted in a diamond pattern (1) are used most often as linings for jackets, snow pants, and vests. Those quilted in a channel pattern of parallel rows (2) are most often used for jackets and vests that are lined with lightweight woven nylon. The filler for most quilted fabrics is polyester fiberfill, which is easy to care for.

Polyester bunting, such as polar fleece (3), retains insulating properties when wet, dries rapidly, and is breathable. This double-faced fabric is easy to sew because it will not ravel. It can be used by itself for unlined jackets, or as a lining to add warmth.

Waterproof & Water Repellent Fabrics

Woven nylon fabrics that have more than one ounce of polyurethane *coating* per square yard offer complete protection from water. These fabrics can be used for garments such as parkas, windbreaker jackets, ponchos, and pullover shells. Among the fabrics that may be coated are ripstop nylon, which has a grid design in its weave, and nylon taffeta, which has a smooth weave and surface sheen.

Belonging in a separate category are *laminated* fabrics, which consist of a waterproof material bonded to another fabric. A durable outer fabric, such as poplin, may be laminated to a nylon tricot on the lining side. This combination makes a strong, lightweight fabric that is breathable, yet waterproof.

Water repellent fabrics are often a more comfortable alternative to waterproof fabrics. Some of the most popular water repellent fabrics are also wind resistant, lightweight, and durable. These include nylon taffeta (4), ripstop nylon (5), and Taslan® nylon (6), which has a distinctive matte surface; mountain cloth (7), which is also called 60/40 because of its nylon/cotton fiber content; tri-blend (8), a comfortable blend of nylon, polyester, and cotton fibers; and densely woven polyester/nylon blends.

Several polyester/cotton blend poplins have been chemically treated for water and stain resistance. These poplins are known for their durability and appealing hand. The finish wears off after repeated launderings, but there are products that can be applied to refresh the water and stain repellency.

Insulations, Linings & Interfacings

The inner layers of a garment may include insulation, lining, and interfacing. In sportwear garments, insulations provide warmth; linings finish the inside of a garment, prevent show-through, ventilate, or add an extra layer for warmth; and interfacings reinforce and stabilize closure areas.

For the inner layers of sportswear, use fabrics that are compatible with the outer fabric; easy care is important. The inner fabric should also meet the needs of the garment. Some patterns, for example, are designed for a nonbulky insulation; others include insulation loft as part of the fashion design.

Thermal insulations trap body heat in tiny air pockets or hollow spaces to keep you warm in low temperatures. For warmth, the insulation is sewn into a garment between the outer fabric and the lining. These insulations are available in three types: thin, high-loft, and needlepunch. All three types are easy to care for but are heat-sensitive, so they should never be pressed with a hot iron.

Thin insulations are available in various weights. Very thin insulation (**1**) of 1.3 oz./sq. yd. (44 g/sq. m) is used for lightweight sportswear in milder climates or for indoor loungewear that requires extra warmth. Midweight insulations of 3.2 oz./sq. yd. (**2**) and 4.9 oz./sq. yd. (**3**) (110 and 165 g/sq. m) are suited for the most active sports, such as cross-country skiing, jogging, and skating. Heavyweight insulation (**4**) of 6.5 oz./sq. yd. (330 g/sq. m) is used for vests, jackets, mittens, slippers, and garments for nonactive outdoor sports, such as hunting and snowmobiling.

High-loft insulations (5) are made from synthetic fibers to resemble down, a natural thermal insulator. The highest loft is the most down-like; the more firmly bonded is the most versatile.

Needlepunch insulations (6) resemble the texture of a blanket. Stretch needlepunch (**7**) has a foam base and is suitable for use with stretch knits.

Thin insulations keep you warm without adding bulk, allowing greater freedom of motion than high-loft and needlepunch. The most widely used contain olefin and polyester microfibers. Thin insulations are ideal for skiwear or other outdoor sportswear that has fitted styling or a soft, draped look; the more fitted the pattern, the more effective the insulation will be. Because thin insulations do not absorb water, they are especially suitable for raingear or for use in a damp climate.

High-loft insulations have qualities similar to down, but they are more affordable, easier to care for, and easier to handle than down. They are quilted or stitched into seams to prevent shifting. High-loft polyester insulations stay warm even when wet.

Needlepunch is made of a polyester fiber base that has been punched with many tiny needles; each needle hole creates an air pocket that helps keep you warm. Needlepunch is less bulky than high-loft insulation and requires no quilting to stabilize it.

Instead of adding thermal insulation to a garment, you can save time by using a prequilted lining. Because prequilted linings add bulk, use a pattern

that is one size larger than usual if the pattern is not designed for a quilted lining. This prevents the fit from becoming too tight.

Garments made from stretch knits are never lined, with the exception of swimwear, which may have a crotch lining or a full-front lining. Self-fabric can be used for a front lining as long as there is no printed or knitted design that will show through the fabric when it is wet. Parkas, vests, and similar outerwear items are lined to make the garment easy to slip on and off, to finish the inside of the garment neatly, to make the garment more water repellent, and to save time spent on raw edge finishes. Usually these garments are lined to the edge, a shortcut sewing technique.

In active sportswear, interfacings are used sparingly. When interfacings are required, their primary function is to strengthen the outer fabric, making the garment more durable. One common place an interfacing is used is underneath a closure, such as a gripper snap or button. Do not use fusible interfacings, because most sportswear fabrics are damaged by a hot iron and steam pressing.

Linings and Interfacings

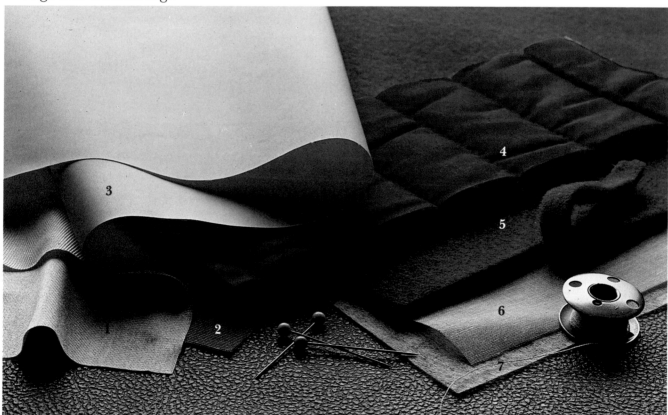

Choose appropriate linings and interfacings. For swimsuits, tricot (**1**) can be used for the crotch lining; two-way stretch knit lining fabric (**2**) can be used for the crotch or full-front lining. Lightweight woven nylon (**3**) is a popular lining fabric, especially when nylon fabric has also been used to sew the outer shell. A prequilted lining (**4**) adds the insulation and lining in one step. Polyester bunting (**5**) is a less bulky alternative to a prequilted lining. To reinforce closures, use sew-in interfacings, either woven (**6**) or nonwoven (**7**).

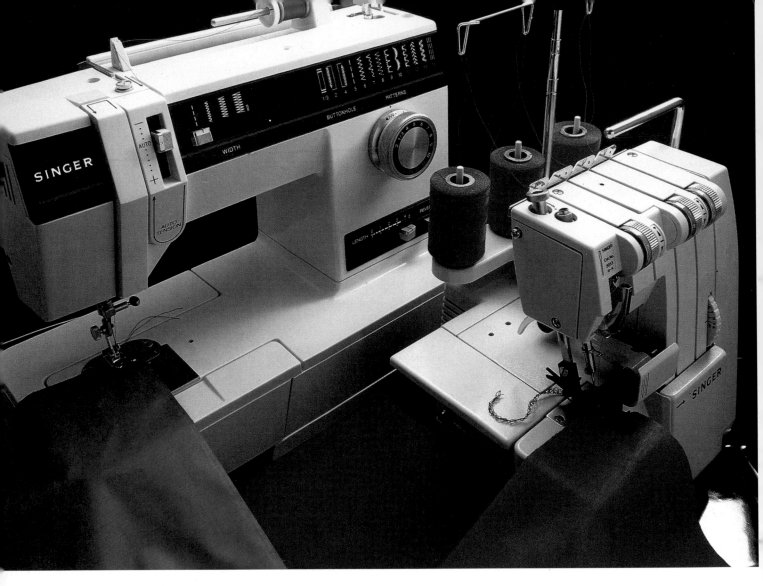

Sewing Equipment, Tools & Supplies

If you have a conventional sewing machine and an overlock machine, set them up side by side for efficient sewing. You will rely solely on machine techniques for sportswear sewing, and you can draw upon the strengths of each type of machine for strong, stretchy seams.

Topstitching, zipper insertions, and buttonholes must be sewn on a conventional sewing machine. You can also sew seams, hems, and edge finishes that resemble those sewn on an overlock if your machine has special stretch and overedge stitch settings. If not, you have the option of using straight and zigzag stitches to achieve a similar result.

The overlock machine, or serger, excels at making narrow edge-finished seams and hems. It trims the seam allowance and overcasts the raw edges as you sew the seam. Slippery nylon fabrics, lightweight stretch knits, and bulky insulations are especially easy to sew on an overlock machine.

Many sportswear fabrics have tight, firm textures, some have chemical coatings, and most are made from synthetic fibers. Stitching problems can occur on such fabrics if your machine is not in good condition. Take the time to clean and lubricate your equipment. Test-sew a scrap of fabric to check the sharpness of the cutting blades in the overlock machine. You may need to replace one or both knife blades if ragged cutting occurs. Synthetic fibers dull blades faster than natural fibers do.

Insert a new needle in each machine and have extra needles on hand. Synthetic fibers and fabric finishes can dull needles quickly, and frequent replacement is necessary for smooth stitching. Select machine needle type according to the fabric you are sewing and use the brand of needle recommended for your sewing machine. To remove the lint residue of synthetic fibers, which can cause stitching problems, wipe the bobbin case and upper tension plates, using a cloth dampened with alcohol. This advance maintenance saves you time and trouble in the long run. Another practical time-saver is to gather the needed tools and supplies before starting a project.

1) **Ballpoint needles** help prevent snags and skipped stitches on two-way stretch knits.

2) **Regular point needles** are used on woven fabrics.

3) **Universal point needles**, which have modified ballpoints, can be used on knits or wovens.

4) **Twin needles** make professional-looking seams and topstitching on actionwear. Twin needles come in different widths; the ⅛" (3 mm) size is suitable for most sportswear applications.

5) **All-purpose sewing thread,** either 100 percent polyester or cotton/polyester, is recommended for most sportswear fabrics.

6) **Overlock thread** is fine and strong for high speed sewing. Most overlock threads are sized between an extra-fine thread and an all-purpose thread.

7) **Woolly nylon thread** helps to make seams softer, stronger, and more elastic. It is sold as an overlock machine thread but can also be wound on the bobbin of a conventional sewing machine for special techniques, such as twin-needle topstitching.

8) **Superfine pins** (.5 mm) should be used on firmly woven nylon, outerwear fabrics, and two-way stretch knits to prevent snagging and pulling.

9) **Weights** can be used instead of pins to hold a pattern in place for cutting.

10) **Glue stick or disappearing basting tape (10a)** can be used instead of basting or pinning to hold trims, pockets, zippers, and insulations in place.

11) **Sharp shears or a rotary cutter (11a)** should be wiped often with a cloth dampened with alcohol to remove lint buildup.

12) **Silicone lubricant** makes it easier to stitch troublesome fabrics.

13) **Liquid fray preventer** locks fabric threads to prevent fraying.

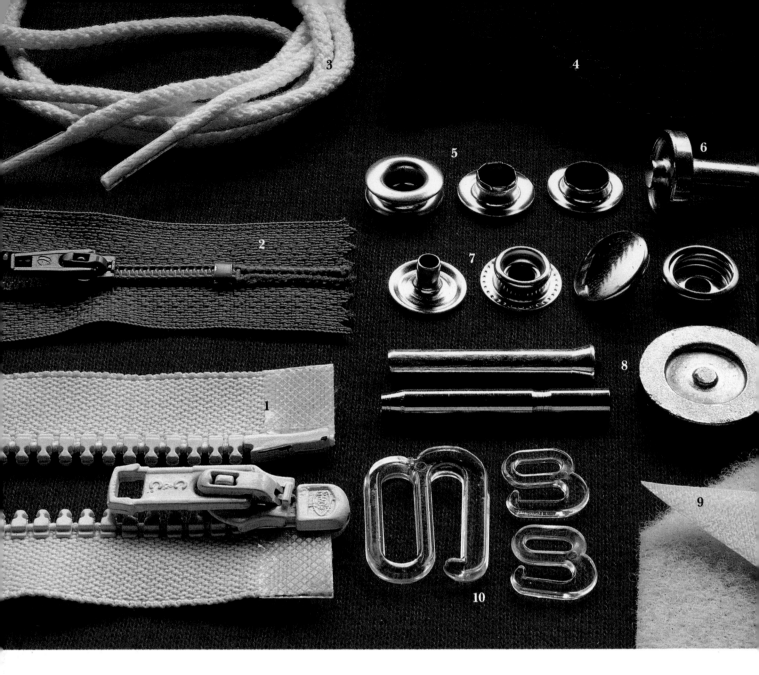

Notions

Some active sportswear items require special notions, such as a windproof closure or a hardy elastic, to perform well under high-stress conditions. Other sportswear garments simply look more professional with the customary trims and hardware, or need authentic sports detailing for the right fashion look.

Closures. A large-toothed zipper with a nylon or polyester coil will not ice up or rust on rugged outerwear; use a separating zipper (**1**) on a jacket or coat. A synthetic coil zipper (**2**) is flexible and supple for lightweight or knit garments. For reversible garments, use a zipper with a pull on both sides of the slider.

For drawstrings, insert round cotton cord (**3**) into a casing; knot or seal raw ends of the cord to prevent raveling if they are not finished. For a lace-up closure, use flat nylon cord (**4**) threaded through grommets (**5**). Grommets can be set into fabric with an easy-to-use tool (**6**) that comes in a kit. Heavy-duty gripper snaps (**7**), which can be used instead of buttons and buttonholes, are applied with a special pliers or a tool included in the package (**8**).

Hook and loop tape (**9**) is a self-sealing, adjustable closure. Use it in addition to or as a substitute for zippers or buttons to make a closure windproof; add the tape to pocket openings to secure contents.

Plastic bra hooks (**10**) are used for swimwear bra closures or neck straps.

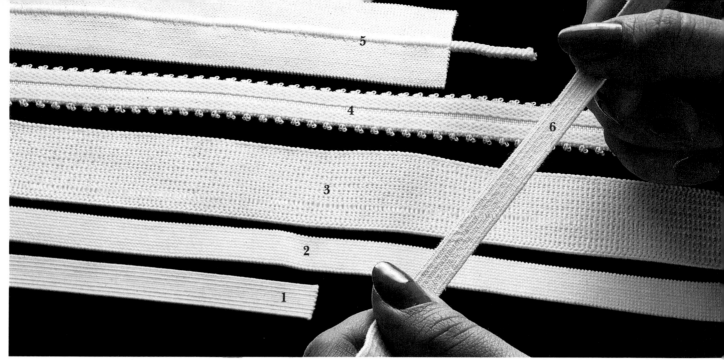

Elastics. Elastics differ in their stretch and recovery characteristics, as well as their suitability for a sewing method. Braided elastic (**1**) narrows when stretched, so it is most often used in a casing. Knitted (**2**) and woven (**3**) elastics retain their original width when stretched. Those made from cotton and rubber are the most durable. Stitch through them for a direct application to fabric. Felt-back or lingerie elastic (**4**) is comfortable when worn next to the skin. Wide elastic (**5**) for actionwear pants and shorts has drawstring for adjustable waistlines. Elastics for swimwear (**6**) have been treated to resist the damaging effects of chlorine and salt and will not lose elasticity when wet.

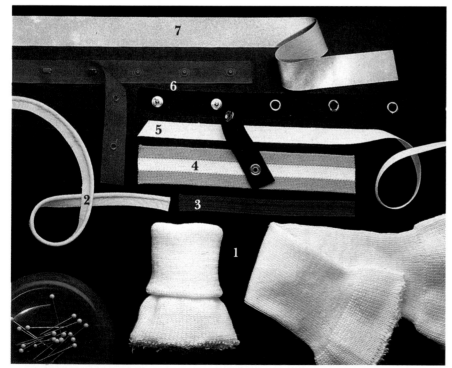

Ribbings, trims, and tapes. Tubular knitted cuffs (**1**) make wrist and ankle edges snug. Piping for decorative seam insertions comes in woven cotton (**2**) and braided nylon blend (**3**). Knitted flat braid (**4**) makes smart-looking striped accents on sweatsuits and fleece jackets. Twill tape (**5**) can be used as a reinforcement for closures or as a rugged-looking trim. Snap tape (**6**) is a sporty trim with metal or plastic snaps attached to twill tape; it is suitable for decorative, low-stress closures. Reflective tape (**7**) adds a measure of safety to garments worn after dusk.

Hardware. To make ties, belts, and straps adjustable, use metal D-rings (**1**) or plastic sliders (**2**); thread snow pants straps through overall buckles (**3**). An alternative fastener for belts and straps is an interlocking buckle (**4**).

Determining Pattern Size

To choose the correct pattern size for women, measure waist, hips, high bust, and bust. Then look at the size chart on the back of a pattern envelope or in a pattern catalog. For garments such as pants, shorts, and tights, select patterns to fit your hips; select all other patterns by your bust measurement. If there is a difference of more than 2" (5 cm) between the full bust and the high bust, you will get a better fit by choosing the pattern according to the high bust measurement.

For men's sizes, use waist measurement to determine pattern size for pants, slacks, and shorts. Use chest measurement for jackets, vests, and shirts.

The major pattern companies adhere to a uniform sizing agreement that is based on average body measurements. This sizing is not the same as ready-to-wear sizing, so do not assume the size for your purchased clothing is correct for patterns.

Many active sportswear patterns are designed for use with specific fabrics, such as two-way stretch knits or quilted fabrics. The amount of ease included in these patterns takes into account the character of the fabric specified, so select your normal pattern size. Patterns for stretch knits, for example, are sized to fit your figure very closely, so the pattern has been scaled down accordingly. Patterns for bulky fabrics such as prequilts will have extra ease for a more comfortable fit. When a pattern states it has been designed for a particular fabric, it may not fit as well if a different fabric is substituted.

Adjusting Pattern Length

Once you have selected the pattern size, shorten or lengthen the pattern as needed to customize the fit. Use your back waist length, inseam, and outseam measurements to determine if length adjustments are needed.

To see if the bodice requires adjustment, compare back waist length with that given for the pattern size on the envelope. If a change is needed, use the adjustment line on the back and front pattern pieces. Do not measure the pattern to compare with body measurements for bathing suits and leotards made of two-way stretch knits. Compare body measurements with the special chart on page 31.

To adjust pants fit, compare inseam and outseam measurements with those given on the pattern envelope for your size. If the pattern envelope gives a finished length measurement, this is the outseam. Measure the pattern piece inner leg to determine the inseam. Make the correct length change on the adjustment lines printed on the pattern or at the lower hem edge.

How to Shorten a Pattern

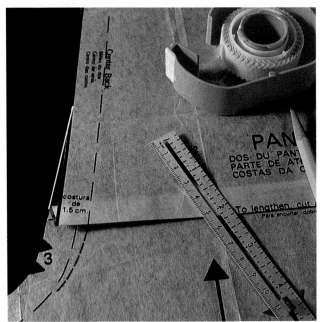

Fold pattern on printed adjustment line to form tuck half as deep as total amount to be removed. Keep depth of tuck uniform and grainline straight. Tape tuck in place, and correct the cutting lines.

How to Lengthen a Pattern

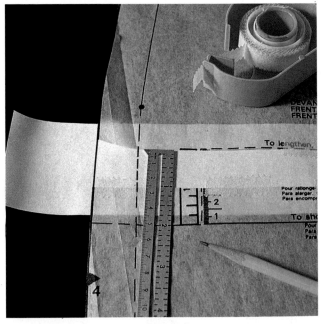

Cut pattern on printed adjustment line. Place extra paper underneath, and spread pattern to add the required length. Keep the grainline straight. Tape pattern to paper, and correct the cutting lines.

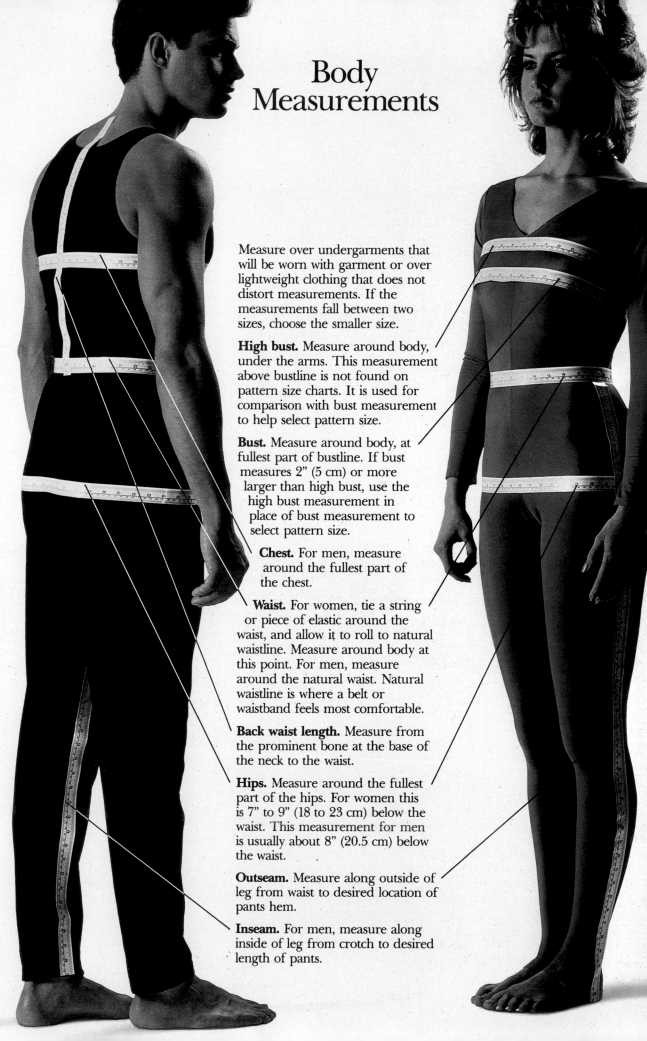

Body Measurements

Measure over undergarments that will be worn with garment or over lightweight clothing that does not distort measurements. If the measurements fall between two sizes, choose the smaller size.

High bust. Measure around body, under the arms. This measurement above bustline is not found on pattern size charts. It is used for comparison with bust measurement to help select pattern size.

Bust. Measure around body, at fullest part of bustline. If bust measures 2" (5 cm) or more larger than high bust, use the high bust measurement in place of bust measurement to select pattern size.

Chest. For men, measure around the fullest part of the chest.

Waist. For women, tie a string or piece of elastic around the waist, and allow it to roll to natural waistline. Measure around body at this point. For men, measure around the natural waist. Natural waistline is where a belt or waistband feels most comfortable.

Back waist length. Measure from the prominent bone at the base of the neck to the waist.

Hips. Measure around the fullest part of the hips. For women this is 7" to 9" (18 to 23 cm) below the waist. This measurement for men is usually about 8" (20.5 cm) below the waist.

Outseam. Measure along outside of leg from waist to desired location of pants hem.

Inseam. For men, measure along inside of leg from crotch to desired length of pants.

Layout, Cutting & Marking

Preshrink most fabrics, tapes, trims, and similar notions, using the laundering method recommended by the fabric manufacturer. Machine wash swimwear knits with warm water and detergent to relax the fabric and remove resins, which may cause skipped stitches. Although swimwear does not shrink, prewashing will return it to its true size. It may have stretched when it was rolled on the bolt. Preshrinking is not necessary for nylon fabrics and chemically coated fabrics because shrinkage is minimal. Do not preshrink thermal insulations or ribbing; they can be damaged by this preliminary step.

When laying out the pattern, avoid placing a pattern piece on the center crease of the fabric, because the crease may be permanent.

Many active sportswear patterns contain multiple sizes printed on the same tissue. To make pattern layout and cutting easier, mark the cutting lines for your size with a felt-tip marking pen. Blend cutting lines from one size into the other if you are using two sizes for one garment.

If you want to use the pattern to cut more than one size, trace it onto wax paper, tissue paper, lightweight nonwoven interfacing, or a gridded nonwoven pattern tracing fabric. Some multiple-size patterns are printed on both sides of the paper, so it is always necessary to trace the pattern pieces onto paper or a see-through interfacing.

Tips for Pattern Layout

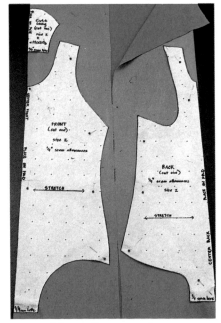

Use "with nap" pattern layout when working with knits and shiny fabrics. Laying all the pattern pieces in the same direction prevents garments from having a two-toned look.

Unfold bulky fabrics such as high-loft insulations and prequilts to lay out on single thickness of fabric. Working with a single layer also helps control slippery fabrics, such as lightweight woven nylons.

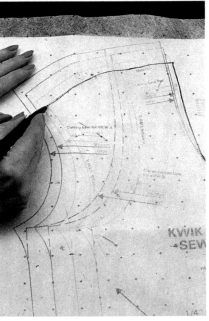

Follow cutting lines for your size when working with multi-sized patterns. Mark correct cutting lines with felt-tip marker for clear cutting guideline, or make a copy of pattern for layout.

Tips for Cutting

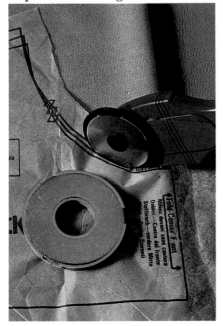

Cut bulky or slippery fabrics easily with rotary cutter. Protect working surface and avoid wear to blade by using plastic mat underneath. Pin in seam allowances only, or use weights to hold pattern in place.

Wipe shears and rotary cutting blades with alcohol to remove lint created by synthetic fibers. Wipe often as you cut, because lint dulls cutting tools. Cleaning method can also be used on pins and sewing machine needles.

Sear uncoated, woven nylon fabrics immediately after cutting to prevent raveling. Hold raw edge tightly, and pass it over lower part of candle flame. When seared correctly, a tiny bead of melted fibers forms a seal.

Marking Techniques

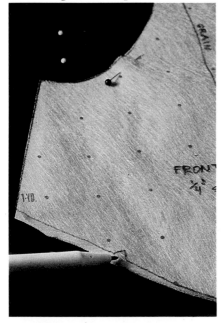

Transfer pattern symbols to fabric, using marking pen with disappearing ink. Mark notches with marking pen or tiny clips. Do not clip into seam allowances of swimwear or uncoated nylon; this may weaken the seams.

Make temporary marks with pins. Insert pins through pattern and fabric at pattern symbols; then carefully lift off pattern. Insert pin in each layer of fabric.

Mark with tailor's chalk if you need longer-lasting symbols than are possible by marking pen or pin methods. Before marking on right side, test to be sure chalk marks can be brushed off.

Stitching Seams & Edges

Commercial patterns vary on the width of pattern seam allowances. Because seam allowances can vary, pay close attention to them on the pattern that you are using. The standard seam allowance of ⅝" (1.5 cm) is used by most pattern companies. Special patterns for swimwear and knit garments may use ¼" (6 mm) or ⅜" (1 cm) seam allowances; some patterns also use ¼" (6 mm) for enclosed seams. Other patterns do not include seam allowances at all; the allowance is added during layout and cutting.

When fitting is not a concern, a one-step method can be used for seams that require trimming to ¼" (6 mm). Cut ¼" (6 mm) seams initially, and you will not have to trim them later. This method is useful for seams where ribbing will be attached and for enclosed seams, such as those for a collar or neckline, which are trimmed to ¼" (6 mm). Make a snip in the seam allowance to remind yourself that it has already been trimmed to the correct width.

Seams and edges on sportswear need to be strong and durable to stand up to activity and stress. To prevent raveling, finish all raw edges of plain seams. Topstitching and edgestitching add strength as well as stylish emphasis to sportswear seams. On knits, use techniques for stretch seams. Twin-needle stitching gives a professional look to sportswear. Use the chart below to select appropriate techniques, needles, and stitches for each fabric.

Guide to Fabrics and Sewing Techniques

Type	Fabrics	Suitable Techniques	Machine Needle	Stitch Length
Lightweight wovens of nylon and nylon blend	Ripstop, taffeta, 60/40, tri-blends	Overlocked, plain, and topstitched seams; seared raw edges of uncoated nylons; overlocked, clean finished, and zigzagged edges	11/75 or 14/90 regular point	8 to 10 per inch (mm setting: 3.5 to 3)
Mediumweight wovens	Taslan® nylon, poplin, twill, gabardine, chino, cotton and cotton-blend plain weaves	Overlocked, plain, and topstitched seams; overlocked, clean finished, and zigzagged edges	14/90 regular point	10 to 12 per inch (mm setting: 3 to 2.5)
Bulky wovens and thermal insulations	Prequilts, needlepunch, high-loft	Overlocked and plain seams; overlocked and zigzagged edges	14/90 or 16/100 regular point	6 per inch (mm setting: 4+) loosen tension
Two-way stretch knits	Swimwear knits and others made from blends with spandex fibers	Overlocked, double-stitched, stretch overedge, and straight stretch seams	11/75 or 14/90 ballpoint	8 to 9 per inch (mm setting: 3.5)
Lightweight knits	Tricot, single knits (jersey, interlock)	Overlocked, double-stitched, and plain seams; zigzagged edges	11/75 or 14/90 ballpoint	12 to 16 per inch (mm setting: 2.5 to 2)
Mediumweight knits	Sweatshirt fleece, velour, stretch terry, sweater knits, double knits	Overlocked, double-stitched, and plain seams; overlocked and zigzagged edges	14/90 ballpoint	12 per inch (mm setting: 2.5)

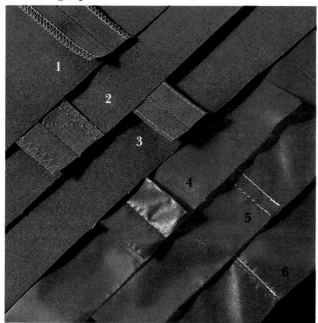

Plain seams. Finish raw edges on an overlock machine (**1**), with a multi-stitch zigzag (**2**), or by clean finishing (**3**). Finish raw edges on nylon by searing (**4**), as shown on page 23. Topstitching (**5**) and edgestitching (**6**) add strength.

Overlock seams. Three-thread overlock stitch (**1**) stretches with fabric and can be used as a seam or edge finish. Four-thread overlock with safety chainstitch (**2**) is strong and stable for wovens but does not stretch on knit seams. Four/three-thread overlock (**3**) has additional line of stitching through the stitch. More stable than three-thread overlock, it has some stretch and can be used on knits.

Stretch seams. On a conventional machine, trim ⅝" (1.5 cm) seam allowances to ¼" (6 mm) before stitching an elastic stretch stitch (**1**). For straight stretch stitch (**2**) or double-stitched seam (**3**), trim after stitching. Double-stitched seam can be sewn with two rows of narrow zigzag (**4**) or a combination of straight and narrow zigzag (**5**).

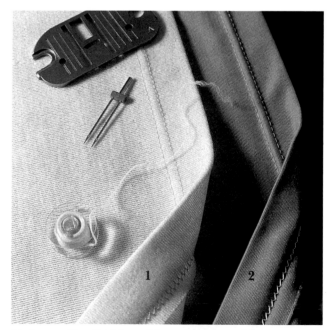

Twin-needle stitching. Most zigzag machines can use the twin needle with a zigzag throat plate. Twin needles give a professional look to sportswear topstitching (**1**). For topstitching on two-way stretch knits, woolly nylon thread (**2**) can be used on the bobbin for extra strength and stretch.

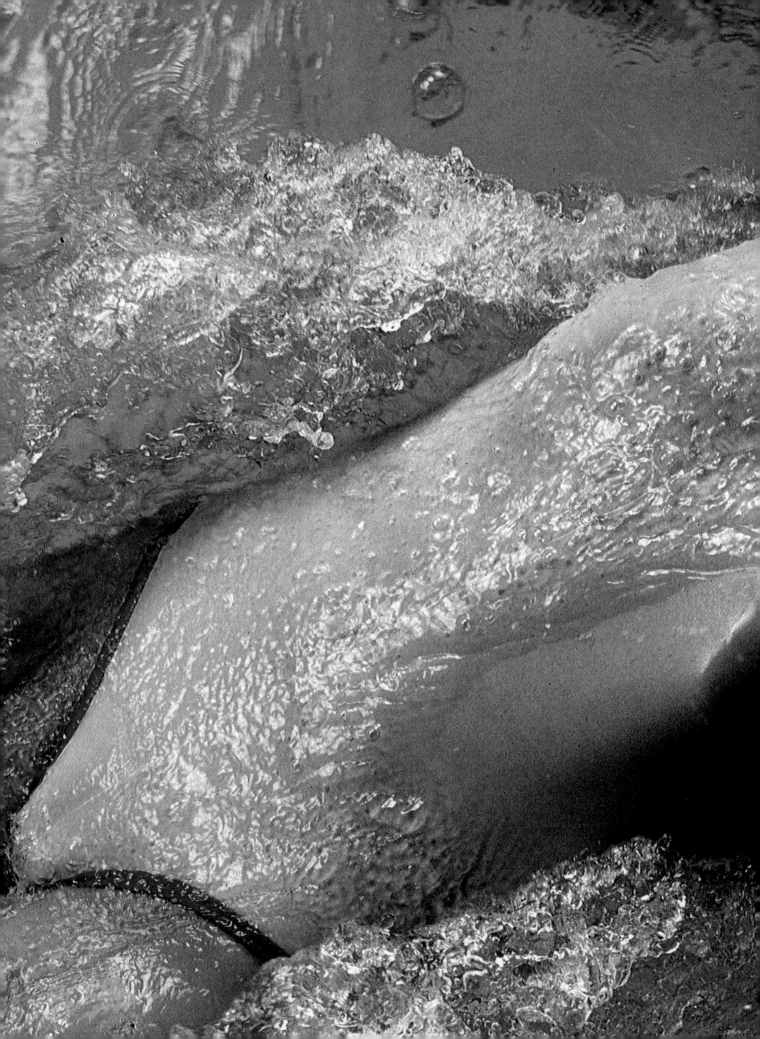

Actionwear

Sewing Actionwear

Patterns for actionwear are usually closely fitted for comfort and easy motion. For competitive sports such as swimming and cycle racing, the style of the garment can even affect the performance during competition. Simple, streamlined styles contribute to the speed of the swimmer or cyclist. Styling details also make a difference. For competitive swimming, choose a swimsuit pattern with criss-crossed or T-style straps, which will not slip off the shoulder.

Be sure to select a pattern specifically designed for a two-way stretch knit. These patterns are sized so the fabric fits snugly without binding or sagging in the finished garment. Woven fabrics will not work.

The pattern envelope defines the amount of stretch that a suitable fabric must have, usually by means of a knit gauge printed on the envelope. Stretch the fabric crosswise and lengthwise to see if it meets the gauge test. Some patterns may specify the percentage of stretch required, such as 100 percent lengthwise stretch and 50 percent crosswise stretch. In this case, stretch a measured amount of fabric against a tape measure or ruler to see if it qualifies. For 100 percent stretch, 4" (10 cm) of fabric must stretch comfortably to 8" (20.5 cm). For 50 percent stretch, 4" (10 cm) must stretch to 6" (15 cm).

Stretch the knit crosswise and lengthwise to determine if the stretch is greater in one direction than the other. Nylon/spandex knits usually stretch more in the lengthwise direction.

For a comfortable fit, swimsuit and leotard patterns specify a pattern layout crosswise on the fabric so the greater stretch encircles the body in the finished garment. On the other hand, patterns for tights, stirrup pants, and unitards require a lengthwise layout so the greater stretch runs vertically, from top to hem in the finished garment. After determining which direction has the greatest amount of stretch, follow the pattern layout guide to position pattern pieces properly.

Fabric Preparation

Although shrinkage of two-way stretch knits is minimal, prewashing has two advantages. It restores the fabric to its original knitted shape if the fabric has become stretched or distorted while rolled on the bolt. It also removes finishing chemicals so the knit is easier to sew. Use the laundering instructions provided by the fabric manufacturer. Allow the fabric to air dry; stretch knits last much longer if not exposed to the heat of machine drying.

How to Use a Knit Gauge

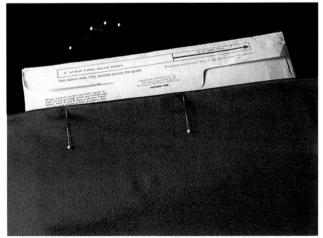

1) Fold edge of knit over about 4" (10 cm), and mark indicated length of relaxed knit with pins. Stretch fold against gauge.

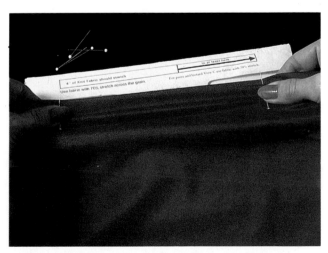

2) Judge the amount of stretch. Correct knit for pattern stretches easily to right-hand side of the gauge. Wrong knit is distorted; stretched edge folds over on itself because of too much stress on fabric.

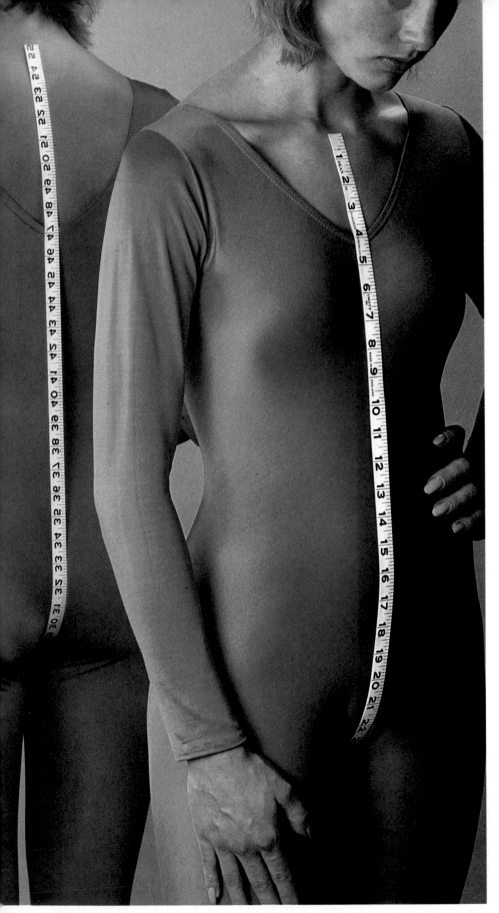

Leotards & Swimsuits

Use two-way stretch knit fabrics for fitted actionwear such as swimsuits, leotards, tights, and unitards (one-piece body suits that combine leotard and tights). Select styles that are practical for the sport and flattering to your figure. Princess seams are slenderizing. So are patterns with a center panel of a contrasting color; to minimize hips, use a dark color for the side panels. High-cut legs on swimsuits and leotards give the appearance of longer legs and a slimmer torso. For a full-busted figure, choose a pattern with a bustline shaped by darts or seams.

To fill out a slender figure, use a pattern with shirring, draping, or ruffles. Or take advantage of the fact that camouflaging is not necessary, and use patterns with high-cut legs or bold cutouts. A simple pattern style sewn in a splashy print is also a way to enhance a slender figure.

One of the benefits of sewing actionwear is making garments to suit your taste and meet your needs, down to the smallest details. You can add a full-front lining to a swimsuit. Build in minimum support at the bust by adding a bandeau lining. A bandeau, an alternative to lining the front, is a straight elasticized lining in the bust area only. For firmer support, purchased bra cups can be added to the bandeau. White or light colors and lightweight knits should be lined because they will become translucent when wet.

Measure from the indentation at the breast bone in front; bring the tape measure between your legs to the prominent bone at the top of your neck in back. Keep the tape measure snug to duplicate the fit of the finished garment.

Fitting & Pattern Adjustments

To keep alterations to a minimum, buy a pattern to fit the bust or high bust measurement. This way you will avoid extensive fitting adjustments; the two-way fabric stretches to fit many different figure shapes. Make length and hip adjustments before cutting.

If you are different sizes in the bust and hip areas, choose a multi-sized pattern, following the cutting lines for the appropriate sizes and blending them at the waistline. For one-piece garments such as swimsuits and leotards, measure your torso length (as shown on opposite page) and compare it to the torso lengths given on the chart at right. Ask someone to help; this is difficult to do by yourself.

If your measurements fall within the range given for your bust size, no pattern adjustment is necessary before you cut. Do not measure the pattern pieces for this comparison because they will measure less than actual body measurements.

If the measurement indicates that you should lengthen or shorten the torso, make the adjustment on the pattern adjustment line on the front and back pattern pieces. If two pattern adjustment lines are indicated on the pattern (above and below the waistline), adjust one-fourth the amount at each adjustment line. Lining will limit the stretch of the knit, so when lining the front of a swimsuit, add 1" (2.5 cm) in overall length; add ½" (1.3 cm) in front and back.

To adjust a leotard or swimsuit pattern for a higher leg cut, draw a new cutting line above the original on the front and back pattern pieces. Begin at the side seam and taper smoothly into the crotch area. Make sure the front and back side seams still match in length. Do not change the width of the pattern in the crotch area. For a lower leg cut, make a similar adjustment on the pattern but draw a new cutting line *beneath* the original.

Comparison of Bust Size with Torso Length

Bust Size	Torso Length
30" (76 cm)	52" to 54" (132 to 137 cm)
32" (81.5 cm)	53" to 55" (134.5 to 139.5 cm)
34" (86.5 cm)	54" to 56" (137 to 142 cm)
36" (91.5 cm)	55" to 57" (139.5 to 145 cm)
38" (96.5 cm)	56" to 58" (142 to 147.5 cm)
40" (102 cm)	57" to 59" (145 to 150 cm)
42" (107 cm)	58" to 60" (147.5 to 152.5 cm)
44" (112 cm)	59" to 61" (150 to 155 cm)

How to Fit Your Torso Length

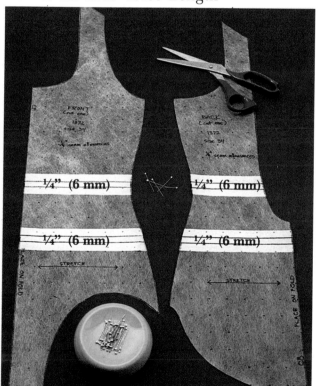

1) Adjust the pattern one-half the needed amount. Example shows adjusting for 2" (5 cm) difference by spreading pattern ¼" (6 mm) on two adjustment lines; to remove length, fold pattern into ⅛" (3 mm) tucks. If pattern has only one adjustment line, make one-fourth of adjustment on front and back.

2) Fit garment after basting side seams and before sewing on elastic. Leave shoulder seams open so they can be adjusted for a snug fit. Adjust leg cut at a length that is flattering to your legs.

Finishing Edges

To stabilize edges and to ensure a snug fit on two-way stretch knit garments, use elastic at necklines, armholes, waistlines, and leg openings. Elasticized edges also allow you to slip the garment on and off easily without adding a zipper or other closure, and they self-adjust to fit your figure. Do not depend on elasticized edges to solve fitting problems. Try on the garment before finishing the edges, and adjust the fit as needed. If a swimsuit is too long, shorten by stitching deeper shoulder seams. If leotard armholes are too small and feel binding, enlarge them by trimming the openings.

If you have not adjusted the neckline, armhole, or leg openings, cut elastic into the lengths specified by the pattern. If you have changed the size of the openings, follow the guidelines given in the chart below. Most patterns print cutting information for elastic on the guide sheet or furnish a cutting guide on the margins of the pattern tissue. If working with a multi-sized pattern, follow the cutting instructions for your size. If using a pattern with several views, be sure to cut the elastic for the style you have chosen; for example, a high-cut leg requires longer elastic than a standard leg style.

Guidelines for Cutting Elastic

Type of Edge	Length to Cut Elastic
Leg opening	Measurement at cut edge of leg opening, minus 2" (5 cm) for adult sizes or 1" (2.5 cm) for children's sizes.
Waistline	Measurement at cut edge of waistline, minus 4" to 6" (10 to 15 cm) according to degree of snug fit desired. Check to see that elastic fits comfortably over hips.
Armhole	Measurement at cut edge of armhole.
Neckline	Measurement at cut edge of neckline. For a snug fit in low, scooped, or V-shaped necklines, use elastic 1" to 3" (2.5 to 7.5 cm) shorter.

How to Apply Elastic

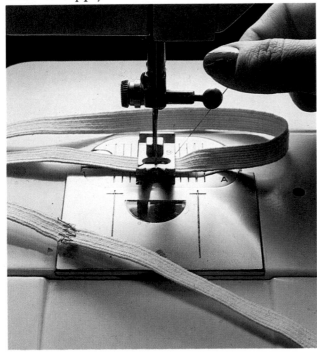

1) Butt ends of elastic, and zigzag or 3-step zigzag to stitch securely. To avoid jamming machine, hold thread ends behind presser foot and make first stitch on length of elastic rather than on cut edge. Backstitch to secure.

2) Divide elastic into fourths, and mark with pins. Place one pin next to ends of elastic. Divide garment edge into fourths, and mark with pins; for neckline or waistline, place one pin at center back and one at center front. Shoulder seams and side seams are not necessarily halfway between centers.

3) Relax elastic when pinning front of leg; then stretch elastic to fit the back. To shape garment to figure contours, stretch elastic as you sew the back of the leg opening.

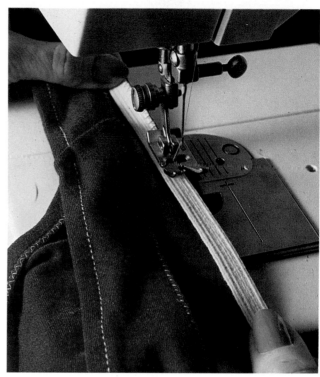

4) Stitch outer edge of elastic to garment, using narrow zigzag stitch. On 3-thread overlock machine, stitch with cutting blades positioned so they will not cut into the elastic.

5) Fold elastic over, toward inside of garment. Elastic is now covered with garment fabric.

6) Lengthen stitches and loosen tension slightly to straight-stitch or narrow zigzag through all layers ¼" (6 mm) from edge; stretch as you sew. Or topstitch with twin-needle straight-stitching, using woolly nylon thread on bobbin.

Elasticized Bindings & Straps

To add a decorative edge finish, use contrasting fabric bindings on swimsuits and leotards. Choose the same stretchy fabric for bindings as used for the body of the garment. Solid colors are effective on printed or striped knits. On striped garments, cut individual stripes of self-fabric for a perfectly matched binding. Cut the binding in the direction of the greatest stretch, usually lengthwise on four-way stretch knit with spandex.

By adapting the elasticized binding method, you can also make stretchy straps or ties easily. The width of the elastic determines the finished width of the strap or tie.

How to Make Elasticized Straps or Ties

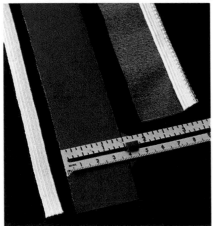

1) **Cut** elastic the finished length of strap or tie, plus allowance for finishing ends. Cut fabric the length of elastic and at least four times the width. Without stretching elastic, zigzag one edge to wrong side of fabric strip.

2) **Fold** elastic over twice, toward wrong side of strip. Pin fabric snugly around elastic.

3) **Stitch** through center of strap. Use twin-needle topstitching or stretch stitch, or use straight stitch and stretch as you sew. Trim excess fabric close to stitches.

How to Finish an Edge with Elasticized Binding

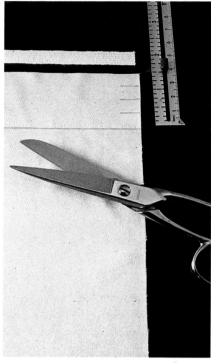

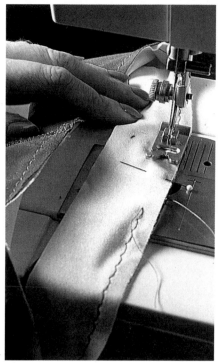

1) Cut binding strip four times the width of the elastic and the length of opening, plus ½" (1.3 cm) for seam allowances. Cut elastic as in elastic guide, page 32.

2) Join ends of elastic as in step 1, page 33. Join ends of binding in ¼" (6 mm) seam. Trim seam allowance (width of elastic) from edge to be bound.

3) Baste right side of binding to right side of garment with long, narrow zigzag stitches ¼" (6 mm) from edge.

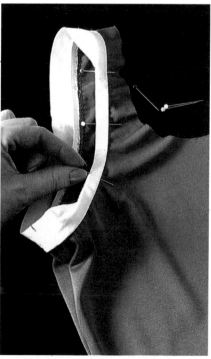

4) Apply elastic, following steps 1 to 3, pages 32 and 33. Stitch inside edge of elastic, using a long, narrow zigzag stitch.

5) Trim binding and garment edge close to stitching. Be careful not to cut into elastic as you trim.

6) Fold binding over elastic to wrong side of garment. Pin as needed. Topstitch through center of binding with twin needle. Trim excess binding on wrong side.

How to Add a Crotch Lining to a Swimsuit

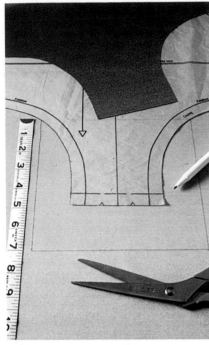  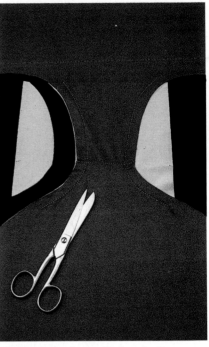

1) Cut crotch lining 7" (18 cm) long and as wide as widest part of crotch area on pattern. Use self-fabric or two-way stretch knit swimwear lining.

2) Stitch crotch seam of swimsuit. Center lining piece over crotch seam of swimsuit with wrong sides together.

3) Machine-baste lining to leg openings, stitching on seamline from right side. Trim off excess lining on sides.

How to Line the Front of a Swimsuit

1) Cut lining, using complete front pattern piece. Use two-way stretch knit swimwear lining fabric. Self-fabric may be used for a solid color; prints or stripes would show through the suit when it is wet.

2) Stitch side and crotch seams of suit. Place right side of lining against wrong side of the suit back; pin side and crotch seams, matching raw edges. Stitch seams a second time. Trim seams to ¼" (6 mm).

3) Turn suit right side out; smooth lining into place inside front of suit. Pin front and lining together; handle as single layer to stitch shoulder seams and to apply elastic (pages 32 and 33).

How to Add a Bandeau Lining

1) Cut bandeau with greater stretch crosswise. For bust sizes 28" to 40" (71 to 102 cm), cut bandeau 8½" by 20" (22 by 51 cm) wide; for sizes 42" to 46" (107 to 117 cm), cut bandeau 11" by 22" (28 by 56 cm) wide. Cut ¾" (2 cm) felt-backed swimwear elastic 2" (5 cm) shorter than bandeau width. Mark center of bandeau, elastic, and swimsuit front.

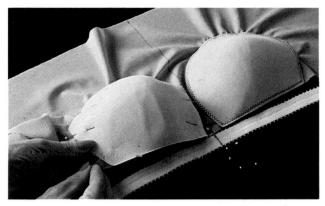

2) Pin bra cups to wrong side of bandeau, one on each side of center mark, with edges of cups and bandeau even. Zigzag-stitch cups to bandeau around entire edge of each cup. If bra cups are omitted, proceed to step 4.

3) Turn bandeau over to right side. Trim away bandeau fabric that falls within zigzag stitching around bra cups.

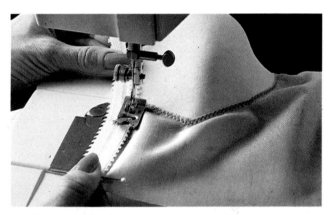

4) Zigzag-stitch elastic to right side of bandeau, matching centers and side edges; stretch elastic to fit. Non-felted side of elastic should face bandeau. Trim excess fabric close to stitching on wrong side.

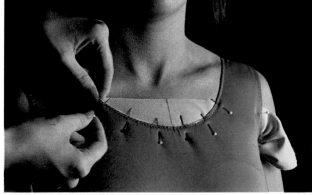

5) Try on swimsuit; pin bandeau in place. Matching centers of bandeau and swimsuit front, smooth bandeau toward neckline and armholes. Remove suit, and adjust placement of pins as needed.

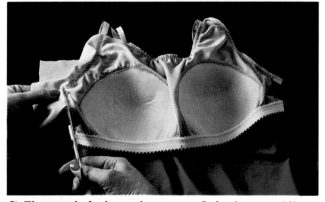

6) Zigzag-stitch through center of elastic at neckline and armholes. Use widest, longest stitch. With short, narrow zigzag, stitch sides of bandeau to swimsuit side seam allowances. Trim excess bandeau fabric. Topstitching secures bandeau at neckline and armholes. Finish attaching elastic (page 33).

Chevroned Stripes

With simple pattern changes, you can add designer details to actionwear. Chevrons, for example, require little more than rotating the printed grainline of the pattern 45 degrees. When the pattern is cut from striped knit, the stripes in the finished garment meet on this bias angle. The result is especially slimming when used on a V-neck swimsuit or leotard pattern.

For chevrons, choose a pattern with a center front and center back seam, or change the foldlines at the center front and back to a seam by adding a seam allowance. Part of a garment, such as sleeves, legs, or yoke, can be chevroned and combined with straight-cut stripes or contrasting solid fabrics for the major garment sections.

How to Adjust and Lay Out a Pattern for Chevroned Stripes

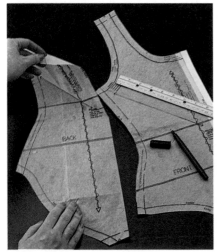

1) Draw new grainline arrow at 45-degree angle to straight grainline arrow on pattern. Draw new arrows on all pieces to be chevroned. If pattern has no center seams, add seam allowance at front and back foldlines.

2) Pin pattern to single layer of fabric, lining up new grainline arrow on one stripe; cut. Flip pattern over to cut right or left-hand section of garment. Match stripes at side seamlines as you position adjoining pattern sections.

3) Pin through edge of stripes to sew perfectly matched seams. Stripes match on the diagonal at the center front, center back, and side seams.

Color Blocking

Color blocking is a creative sewing technique used to add distinctive style to actionwear or to custom-make competitive outfits in team colors. Color blocking involves cutting the pattern apart and adding seam allowances to the new cutting lines to form inserts of one or more contrasting fabrics. This detailing is most suitable for simply styled garments, such as cycling shirts, leotards, tank-style and maillot swimsuits, and unitards. To complement color blocking, you can also use contrasting fabric for sleeves, yokes, and ribbings.

How to Add Color Blocking to a Pattern

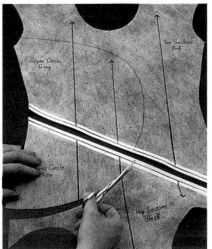

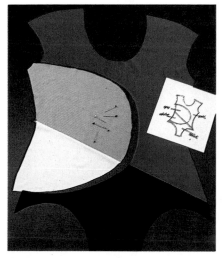

1) Extend grainline arrow to edges of pattern piece, using ruler to keep grainline arrow straight as you draw. Divide pattern piece into sections by drawing new seamlines where desired.

2) Label sections of pattern; cut pattern apart on new seamlines. Tape paper underneath to add ¼" (6 mm) seam allowance on both edges, drawing new cutting lines for pattern sections.

3) Cut pattern sections as desired from contrasting fabrics. Stitch color-blocked garment sections together first. Then complete the garment, following the pattern guide sheet.

Hems

Hems for actionwear are quick and easy to sew because knit fabrics do not ravel. Use a cut edge, edgestitching, lettuce edging, or mock-cuff hem.

Cut edge is the quickest and easiest hem of all. Because this no-sew method of cutting the edge at the hemline produces a single-layer finish, it eliminates bulk and encourages a graceful flow of fabric on full skirts or ruffles.

Edgestitching makes a neat, narrow hem for wrap knit skirts or the lower edge of tights that do not

have elastic. It does not add the weight of a deep hem or interfere with the stretch of the knit fabric.

Lettuce edging, shown above, gives a decorative three-dimensional look to skating skirts and other garments with ruffles or fullness. This hem can be stitched with an overlock or narrow zigzag stitch.

Mock-cuff hem is similar to a blindstitched hem but gives the look of a cuff, even though it is actually a turned-up hem stitched on the inside. The mock cuff is ideal for straight edges. Like lettuce edging, it can be stitched with an overlock or narrow zigzag stitch.

Four Ways to Hem Stretch Knits

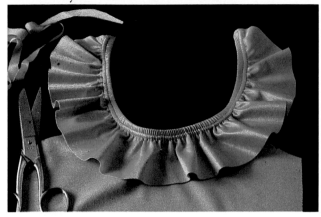

Cut edge. Trim garment neatly on hemline. Use sharp shears and cut with long, firm strokes. When edge becomes worn, trim a slight amount to renew the fresh look. Clean-cut edge works best on firm knits, which will not fray.

Edgestitching. Turn under hem allowance, and edgestitch; then on inside of garment, trim excess hem allowance close to edgestitching. Use short straight stitch for this neat, narrow hem, and do not stretch fabric as you sew.

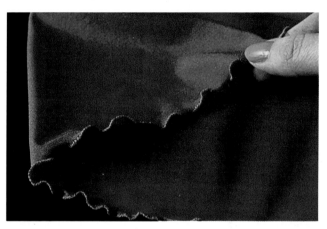

Lettuce edge. Trim garment on hemline. Use a closely spaced zigzag stitch over the cut edge of fabric, positioning edge at center of foot. Stretch hem as you sew; the more you stretch the fabric, the more ruffled the edge will be.

Lettuce edge on an overlock machine. Use the rolled hem setting. Stretch hem as you sew; the more you stretch the fabric, the more ruffled the edge will be.

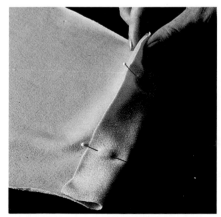

Mock-cuff hem. 1) Fold hem up; then fold hem back toward right side of garment into position for blind hemming.

2) Stitch just to the left of the top fold, using an overlock stitch or narrow zigzag. Remove pins as you come to them.

3) Open hem out. Do not press flat; slight roll between garment and hem gives appearance of an attached cuff.

Tights

Because of their warmth and comfortable fit, tights have long been standard attire for dance, aerobics, and other indoor exercise activities. More and more they have also become popular accessories for outdoor sports such as running and biking. Custom-made tights can be made footless or with stirrups. A practical slimline style is the unitard, a one-piece design that combines leotard and tights. For a layered look, coordinate actionwear leotard and tights, and add any combination of T-shirt, sweatshirt, shorts, or leg warmers for warmth or style.

For stirrup tights or pants, comfortable length is especially important. With proper fit the pants are stretched taut enough lengthwise to be smooth and wrinkle-free but long enough to be comfortable for moving and bending. To fit the length more

accurately, add 1" to 2" (2.5 to 5 cm) to the waistline and lower edge of the stirrups, and stitch the stirrups only after you have assembled the tights. Make adjustments in length after trying on the pants and bending and stretching to check for comfort.

For footless tights, cut off the stirrup extension, allowing ½" (1.3 cm) for hemming. For a longer leg-warmer look, add 2" to 6" (5 to 15 cm) at the lower edge; push the tights leg up into soft folds above the ankle.

To fit a unitard, use the torso length chart for swimsuits and leotards for the upper body (page 31). Measure the torso length. If adjustments are necessary, make them above and below the waistline.

How to Sew Stirrup Tights

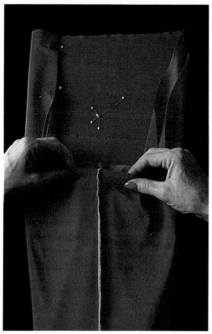

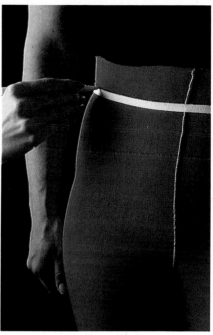

1) Stitch inseam of each leg. Serge, or use double-stitched narrow zigzag seam, stretching as you sew. Use woolly nylon thread on the serger for extra strength.

2) Slip one leg inside the other with right sides together. Serge or zigzag-stitch crotch seam from front to back in one continuous curve.

3) Lap and stitch ends of waistline elastic. Try on tights, wrong side out with waist elastic in place. Mark tights along upper edge of elastic. Remove tights and elastic. Turn tights right side out.

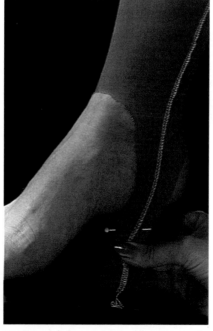

4) Stitch elastic on wrong side with edge of elastic above marked line, stretching elastic to fit. If using zigzag, trim excess fabric above waistline. Fold elastic to wrong side. With wide zigzag, stitch through all layers; stretch elastic as you sew.

5) Turn tights wrong side out, and try on to determine placement of instep seam. Pin both seams; test comfort by bending and stretching. After adjusting fit, stitch the instep seams securely.

6) Finish curved stirrup openings at bottom of tights with serging, narrow hem, or 3-step zigzag. This creates neat, nonbulky edges.

Bicycling Shorts & Shirts

Stretch knit separates for bike touring and racing feature streamlined, close-to-the-body styling to provide ease of movement and to cut down on wind resistance. Specialty patterns are available for biking shirts and shorts. Purchase these patterns through mail-order firms or modify similar patterns by adding the high-performance details shown on the following pages. With either type of pattern, use a durable, two-way stretch knit with spandex combined with nylon, polypropylene, or wool.

Biking shorts are close fitting and cut to a finished length about 2" (5 cm) above the knee. The waistline fits the natural waist in front but is contoured about 3" (7.5 cm) higher than the natural waistline across

the back. Waist and leg openings are elasticized for fit and comfort.

Crotch padding is an important feature of biking shorts. This protective detail can be cut from polyester bunting fleece, a fabric readily available for sewing.

For smooth fit and good coverage when in cycling position, cyclists prefer shirts cut about 3" (7.5 cm) longer in back so the back hem is 9" to 10" (23 to 25.5 cm) below the waist. The front hem falls 6" to 7" (15 to 18 cm) below the waist. To adapt a pattern for biking, you may have to add length to the back and sides and reshape the hemline.

Pattern Pieces for Cycling Shorts

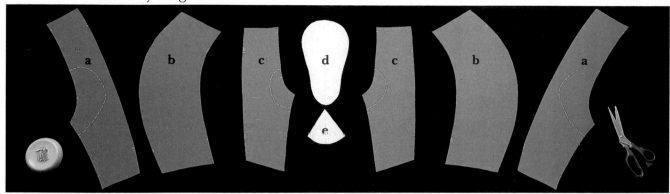

Six panels shape cycling shorts for maximum fit and comfort. Back **(a)** has extra length to accommodate bent-over cycling position. Side panels **(b)** are shaped for close-to-the-body fit. Shorts front **(c)** is 3" (7.5 cm) shorter than the back. Center padding panel **(d)** is cut from polyester bunting fleece. Wedge insert **(e)** for padding adds shape: Mark notches and centers of panel and wedge.

How to Sew Crotch Padding in Cycling Shorts

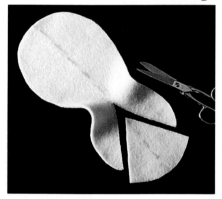

1) Slash center panel on marked line up to pattern notch.

2) Insert center wedge so edges butt against slashed opening in center panel. Stitch wedge to panel, using wide zigzag stitches.

3) Stitch center front, back, and inseam with stretch stitch or double-stitched seams; stretch as you sew. Or serge with 3-thread overlock stitch.

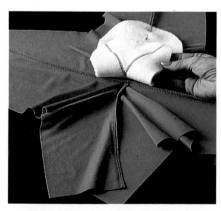

4) Open shorts out flat, wrong side up. Place padding over crotch seam, with wedge toward front. Match point of wedge with intersection of seams; pin point in place. Align padding center marks with front and back seams; pin.

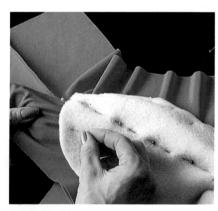

5) Pin the edges of padding to shorts, stretching the knit fabric ¼" to ½" (6 mm to 1.3 cm) to fit the shaped padding.

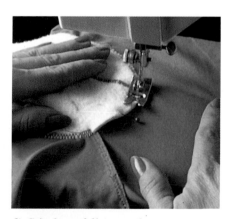

6) Stitch padding to shorts, stretching fabric slightly as you sew. Use wide zigzag to catch cut edge of padding completely. To secure, overlap stitching at beginning and end.

How to Finish Elasticized Edges on Bicycle Shorts

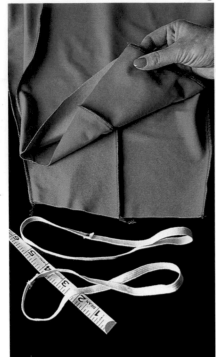  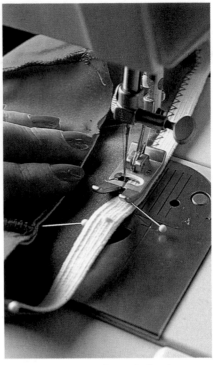

1) Stitch side seams of shorts. Cut ⅜" (1 cm) wide elastic the length of each leg opening, plus ½" (1.3 cm) for seam allowances. Lap ends of elastic ½" (1.3 cm), and zigzag-stitch securely.

2) Trim leg hem allowance to ⅜" (1 cm). With garment inside out, slip elastic inside leg, and line up with raw edge of shorts. Elastic is on right side of fabric.

3) Stitch inner edge of elastic to shorts leg, using wide zigzag stitch. Position needle so it swings past edge to allow only half the stitches to pierce elastic.

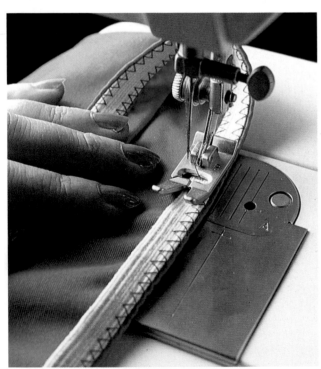 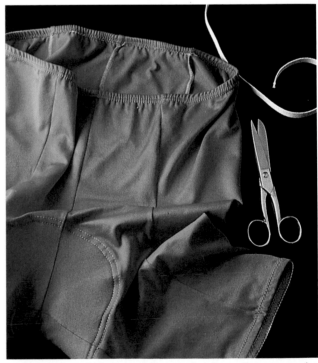

4) Turn shorts right side out. Fold elastic to inside of leg opening. Stitch free edge of elastic with wide zigzag stitch. Position elastic so needle swings past edge, as in step 3.

5) Cut ⅜" or ½" (1 or 1.3 cm) elastic to fit your waist measurement, plus ½" (1.3 cm) for seam allowances. Apply to shorts waistline as for elasticized edge (pages 32 and 33).

How to Make a Back Pocket on a Bicycle Shirt

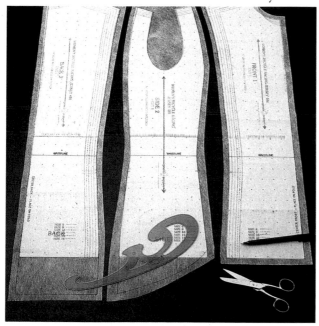

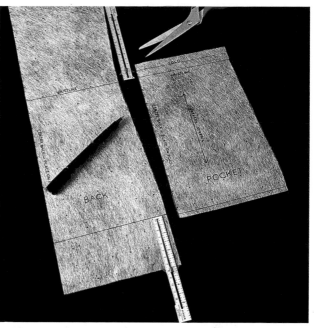

1) Adjust pattern by adding 3" (7.5 cm) to back and side panels. Taper cutting line back into original cutting line at side front. Shaped hem fits smoothly and provides good coverage when in cycling position.

2) Cut pocket to fit across back panel, using back pattern. Finished lower edge of pocket is 3" (7.5 cm) above hem; finished top edge is ½" (1.3 cm) above waist marking. Add ½" (1.3 cm) seam allowance to top of pocket and ¼" (6 mm) to bottom. Greater knit stretch should run from pocket top to bottom.

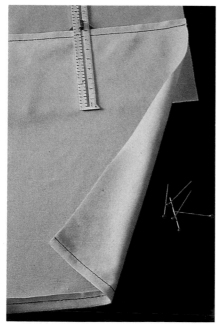

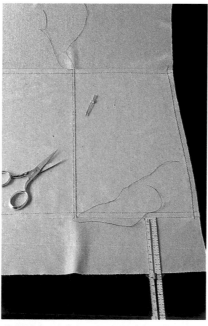

3) Fold ½" (1.3 cm) under on top edge of pocket, and topstitch. With right sides together, place lower edge of pocket 3¼" (8.2 cm) above hemline. Pocket is upside down. Before sewing side seams, stitch pocket to shirt ¼" (6 mm) from raw edge.

4) Fold pocket up. Machine-baste sides of pocket to side seams. Topstitch ¼" (6 mm) from seam at lower edge. Stitch through pocket and shirt to divide pocket into two or three sections, beginning at bottom of pocket. Shorten stitch length near top, pull threads to wrong side, and tie to secure.

5) Fold hem up ½" (1.3 cm). Topstitch or straight-stitch with double needle ⅜" (1 cm) from fold, using 8 to 10 stitches per inch (3.5 to 3 mm stitch setting). Stretch fabric slightly as you sew.

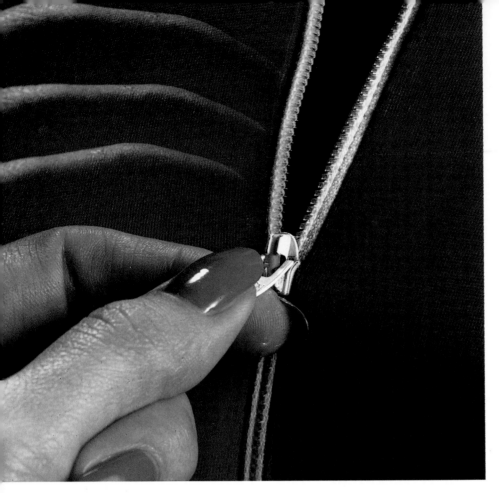

Zippers in Stretch Knits

Most two-way stretch knit garments are pull-on styles and do not need a zipper or other closure; however, when garments such as unitards, leotards, bicycling shirts, or skating dresses have high, fitted necklines, a zipper is necessary.

The following method for inserting a zipper on stretch knit garments can be used at the center back or center front even if there is not a seam there. A layer of lightweight sew-in interfacing stabilizes the fabric in the zipper area for a smooth, even, nonbulky closure. Use a lightweight synthetic coil zipper for best results.

How to Insert a Zipper in a Stretch Knit Garment

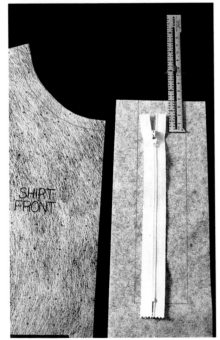

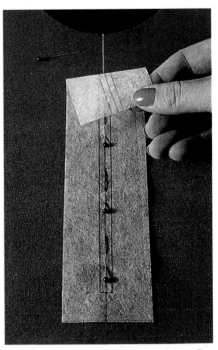

1) Determine the length of zipper opening by measuring the zipper between bottom and top stops, then adding pattern seam allowance. Cut lightweight nonwoven sew-in interfacing 2" (5 cm) wide and 1" (2.5 cm) longer than zipper.

2) Mark total length of zipper opening in center of interfacing. Draw a stitching box ¼" (6 mm) wide with marked length through center of box. Mark zipper opening on right side of garment.

3) Pin interfacing to right side of garment, centering stitching box where zipper will be inserted. Match interfacing center mark to zipper marking on garment.

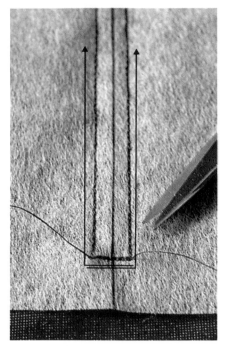  

4) Stitch across bottom of box, pivot, and stitch up one side of box. Use short stitch, about 15 per inch (2 mm stitch setting). Repeat on other side, stitching in direction of arrows. To prevent stitches from piling up, do not backstitch.

5) Slash through center of stitching box, clipping diagonally to each corner. Do not cut into stitches. Turn interfacing to wrong side. Press with cool iron, rolling seam to wrong side.

6) Use basting tape to baste zipper behind opening. Position bottom stop of zipper exactly at bottom of opening; place sides of opening next to zipper teeth.

  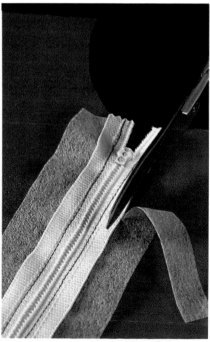

7) Lift garment up, and fold one side over to expose zipper tape and interfacing. Stitch across triangle at bottom of zipper tape, pivot, then stitch up exposed side. Stitch over previous stitching.

8) Fold other side of garment back to expose remaining side of zipper tape and interfacing. Again, stitch across bottom of zipper tape, pivot, and stitch up exposed side, stitching over previous stitching.

9) Trim interfacing close to edges of zipper tape. In completed insertion, zipper teeth are exposed and no stitches show from the right side.

Comfortwear

Sewing Sportswear for Comfort

Rugby shirts, running shorts, T-shirts, and warm-up suits are designed for active sports comfort but have also become fashion items. One of the reasons for their popularity is their comfort. These garments are usually made of soft knit fabrics and have snug-fitting ribbed, drawstring, or elasticized edges for even greater comfort.

Pullover sweatshirts and pull-on pants are easy to sew because there are few pattern pieces, all the sewing is done by machine, and the construction can be simplified by the use of flat methods (pages 56 and 57). Fitting for active sportswear is minimal. Patterns usually come in small, medium, large, and extra-large sizes rather than the more specific numbered sizes necessary for other garments. Simple length adjustments (pages 20 and 21) are usually all that is required for loosely fitted sportswear patterns.

With some sewing experience, you can also create professional-looking rugby and polo shirts, tank tops, and split-leg running shorts. Or you can add optional details to simple pattern styles. Consider the alternative waistbands suitable for sweatpants. Try an expandable pocket for tennis shorts. Iron-on trims and appliqués personalize a basic design.

Fabric Preparation

Preshrink fabrics, tapes, and trims. Preshrink notions to prevent edges and detail areas from rippling in the finished garment. Use the washing and drying methods recommended by the fabric's manufacturer. Do not preshrink ribbings. This distorts ribbing and makes accurate layout and cutting difficult.

Preshrinking the fabric restores the original shape of knits such as sweatshirt fleece and velour, preventing twisted seams in the finished garment. Washing also removes chemical finishes and excess dyes from knits and makes the fabrics easier to sew.

After preshrinking, knits may ripple or look uneven along the selvage edges. To prepare the fabric for pattern layout, fold it along a lengthwise rib and smooth out any wrinkles. It is important to align the pattern sections on the straight grain of the fabric. If sections are cut off-grain, the finished garment will twist instead of draping properly.

Ribbings

Ribbing has lengthwise ridges with great crosswise stretch and recovery, enabling the ribbing to return to its original size and shape. Because of its stretch and recovery qualities, ribbing may be used instead of a hem to finish necklines, wrists, ankles, armholes, and waistlines. Ribbed edges provide a snug but comfortable fit for pullover and pull-on garments.

Purchasing Ribbings

Most ribbings are sold by the inch (centimeter) in tubular form. A typical ribbing is 22" (56 cm) wide. Polyester/cotton ribbings (1) are a suitable choice for sweatshirt fleece, lightweight jersey, and T-shirt knits. For outerwear, nylon/spandex ribbing (2) provides a firmer, stronger edge. These tubular ribbings are cut to the correct length for the garment. Because the ribbing is folded crosswise to finish the outer edge, it is cut twice the finished width.

For casual knit shirts, use a ribbing set (3) for the collar and the sleeve edges; the set, which is usually striped in one or two additional colors, has finished outer edges. For dressier knit garments, finished edge ribbing (4) is sold by the yard (meter). It is

a single layer of ribbing to be cut to size for the specific garment. Ready-made cuffs (5) in doubled tubular form eliminate the need to fit the ribbing to the garment. The fold forms the finished edge.

Because the color selection of ribbings may be limited, a contrasting ribbing is often a more attractive choice than striving for a perfect match. You could also substitute other fabrics, such as two-way stretch spandex knit, for ribbing, as long as the fabric has good stretch and recovery qualities. Also, you can cut self-fabric strips crosswise if working with a knit that stretches at least 25 percent in this direction.

Cutting Ribbings

Ribbings vary in their amount of stretch, so it is best to estimate the length of ribbing required either by pin-fitting it on your body or by measuring the garment edge. The finished width should be in proportion to the size of the garment edge. For example, waistline ribbings are cut wider than ribbings for necklines and sleeveless armholes.

Cut ribbing from a single thickness, or fold it crosswise and cut it doubled as it will be applied to the garment. Lightweight ribbings are easier to handle if folded and pressed lightly before cutting; be careful not to stretch the ribbing while pressing. The chart on page 54 provides measurements for cutting folded and unfolded ribbings.

Sewing Techniques for Ribbings

To apply ribbings to a garment edge, use either the flat or tubular method. For a flat method, leave one seam open; apply ribbing to the garment after sewing only one shoulder seam for a neck ribbing, or one side seam for a waistline ribbing. When the other shoulder or side seam is sewn, the ends of the ribbing are joined in the seam. A serged seam is ideal for the flat method because the raw edges of the ribbing are finished as you sew. Apply ankle ribbing after sewing the outseam of pants. Apply sleeve ribbing before sewing the underarm seam.

For a tubular or "in-the-round" method, the garment and ribbing ends are seamed separately. The application allows you to position the ribbing seam in an inconspicuous place such as the center back. For a better quality finish, it also encloses the raw edges where the ribbing ends are seamed.

Guide to the Finished Width and Cut Size of Ribbings

Type of Garment Edge	Finished Width	Cut Size (unfolded, including seam allowances)	Cut Size (for finished-edge ribbing)
Sleeveless armhole	¾" to 1" (2 to 2.5 cm)	2" to 2½" (5 to 6.5 cm)	1" to 1¼" (2.5 to 3.2 cm)
Short sleeve	1" (2.5 cm)	2½" (6.5 cm)	1¼" (3.2 cm)
Long sleeve for shirt or jacket	2" to 3" (5 to 7.5 cm)	4½" to 6½" (11.5 to 16.3 cm)	2¼" to 3¼" (5.7 to 8.2 cm)
Crew or V-neckline	1" to 1¼" (2.5 to 3.2 cm)	2½" to 3" (6.5 to 7.5 cm)	1¼" to 1½" (3.2 to 3.8 cm)
Shirt or jacket waistline	2½" to 3" (6.5 to 7.5 cm)	5½" to 6½" (14 to 16.3 cm)	2¾" to 3¼" (5.7 to 8.2 cm)
Pants waistline	2½" to 3" (6.5 to 7.5 cm)	5½" to 6½" (14 to 16.3 cm)	Not suitable for pants
Pants leg cuff	3" (7.5 cm)	6½" (16.3 cm)	3¼" (8.2 cm)

How to Estimate the Cut Length of Ribbing

Pin-fit ribbing around body for straight edges such as wrists, waistline, short sleeves, or ankles. Fold ribbing crosswise for double thickness. Ribbing should lie flat without gaping. Do not distort ribs. Add ½" (1.3 cm) for seam allowances.

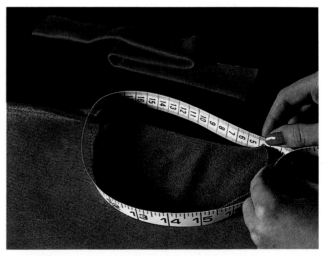

Measure cut edge for necklines and armholes. Trim seam allowance to ¼" (6 mm). Stand tape measure on end to determine length accurately. Cut ribbing two-thirds measured length of garment edge, plus ½" (1.3 cm) for seam allowances. For V-neckline, cut ribbing the same measurement as the garment.

How to Apply Ribbing (tubular method)

1) Join ribbing ends in ¼" (6 mm) seam; fold in half lengthwise, wrong sides together. Divide ribbing into fourths, and mark with pins; place one pin at seam. Divide garment edge into fourths, and mark with pins; place a pin at center back and center front.

2) Match pin markers of ribbing to garment; pin, placing ribbing seam at center back.

3) Stitch ¼" (6 mm) seam with ribbing on top, garment on bottom, using overedge stretch stitch, narrow zigzag, or overlock. Stretch ribbing to fit garment edge between each set of pins. Press seam toward garment.

How to Apply Ribbing (flat method)

1) Divide ribbing into fourths; mark with pins. Divide garment edge into fourths; mark with pins.

2) Pin ribbing to garment, matching pins. Serge, or use narrow zigzag to stitch ribbing to right side of garment in ¼" (6 mm) seam. Stretch ribbing to fit garment edge as you sew.

3) Stitch garment seam, starting at ribbing edge; match ends of ribbing and ribbing seam carefully by placing pin through center of stitching lines. Backstitch to secure seam if using straight stitching.

Sweatsuits & Warm-ups

Sweatsuits and warm-ups consist of a sweatshirt or jacket and pull-on pants. Sweatsuits for sports activities are usually made of cotton or cotton/polyester knit fleece. Warm-ups are worn for warming up during the first few minutes of sports activity and for keeping warm after the activity or exercise. Design features of sweatsuits and warm-ups also make them popular for casualwear.

How to Sew a Sweatshirt (flat method)

1) Stitch one shoulder seam, using double-stitched seam or overedge stitch. Or serge the seam on an overlock machine.

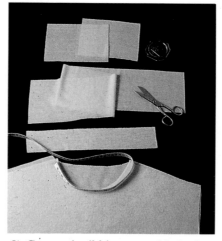

2) Cut neck ribbing two-thirds the distance around neckline, plus ½" (1.3 cm) for seam allowances. Cut ribbing for waist and wrists to fit body comfortably, plus ½" (1.3 cm) for seam allowances.

3) Apply neck ribbing, using flat method (page 55). Stitch other shoulder seam, beginning stitching at neckline edge; backstitch or secure ends of thread.

4) Pin sleeves to shirt, matching pattern symbols at shoulder seams. Stitch sleeve seams. Leave underarm seams unstitched.

5) Apply wrist ribbings, using flat method, page 55. Stitch one underarm seam, right sides together. Leave one side open.

6) Apply waist ribbing, using flat method, page 55. Stitch remaining underarm seam.

V-Necklines

A V-neckline is a classic neck edge, and on activewear garments it is commonly finished with ribbing. The lapped method is the quickest technique for applying the ribbing.

For the lapped method, cut the ribbing to an estimated generous length to start. Stretch the ribbing slightly along the front of the neckline; stretch it to a greater degree across the back. When you near the end of the stitching, you know exactly how much excess ribbing to trim off. This measure-as-you-sew technique results in a ribbed edge that lies snug and flat against the body.

For a woman's garment, lap the ribbing toward the left-hand side. For a man's garment, lap the ribbing in the opposite direction; stitch the left-hand side of the ribbing first, and then lap the ribbing toward the right-hand side.

How to Apply Lapped Ribbing to a V-Neckline

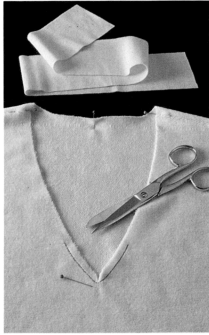

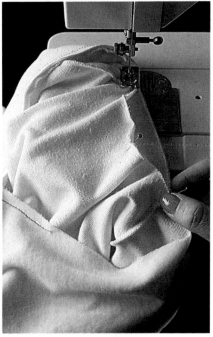

1) Cut ribbing slightly longer than the cut edge of neckline. With short stitches, staystitch on the seamline 2" (5 cm) on either side of the V. Clip carefully to the V. Fold ribbing in half lengthwise.

2) Pin ribbing to right-hand side of neckline in ¼" (6 mm) seam; leave 1" (2.5 cm) for lapping. With garment on top, begin stitching at center front. Stretch ribbing slightly as you sew.

3) Stop stitching at shoulder seam. Measure back neckline between shoulder seams. Mark ribbing with pin at point equal to two-thirds the measured length. Match pin mark to shoulder seam.

4) Stitch ribbing to garment across back neckline and down left-hand side of neckline, stretching ribbing slightly. Stop stitching before reaching point of V, leaving an opening equal to width of ribbing. Remove garment from machine.

5) Turn ribbing seam to inside. Lay garment out flat. Tuck the extensions inside the seam opening with right-hand side overlapping left. Pin ribbing at center front in lapped position.

6) Fold front of garment out of the way. From wrong side, stitch opening closed; pivot at point of V, and stitch free end of ribbing to right-hand seam allowance. Trim extensions close to stitches.

Waistline Finishes

Sweatpants or warm-up pants are simple to sew because they have only two major pattern pieces and the fit at the waistband is adjustable. There are several ways to finish pants at the waistline. None of the techniques is difficult, but they may require adapting the pattern by marking new cutting lines above the waistline.

Elastic in a casing is a simple and easy waistline finish. Elastic 1" or ¾" (2.5 or 2 cm) wide is normally used in the casing.

Ribbing waistband with a drawstring or elastic is less bulky and more comfortable than a casing. Ribbing of a contrasting color is decorative as well as practical.

Elastic with built-in drawstring is 1½" (3.8 cm) elastic knitted with a flat cord running through its center. It is generally sold on rolls in fabric stores.

Casing with multiple rows of elastic does not twist or roll. Three rows of ½" (1.3 cm) elastic create a waistband slightly wider than most elasticized casings. For a narrower waistband, use two rows of elastic instead of three.

Elasticized waistband with several rows of stitching is a comfortable, non-roll finish for knit sweatpants or nylon warm-ups. Elastic applied with this method will not twist or shift. Use elastic with good stretch and recovery qualities so the waistband retains its fit. As an option, you can add a drawstring.

How to Sew Pants with Elastic in the Casing

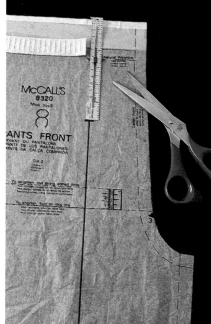

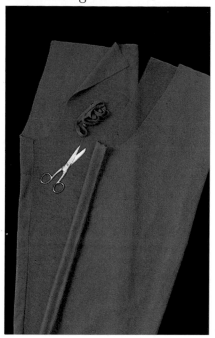

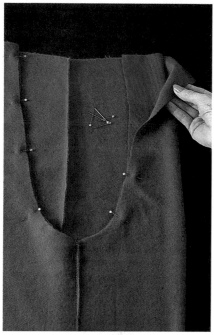

1) Mark casing on pattern, above waistline. Allow twice the width of elastic, plus ½" (1.3 cm). For example, mark 2½" (6.5 cm) casing for 1" (2.5 cm) wide elastic. Cut elastic to fit waist comfortably, plus ½" (1.3 cm) seam allowance.

2) Stitch leg seams on pants, right sides together. Use conventional straight stitch or narrow zigzag stitch, and trim seam allowances to ¼" (6 mm). Or serge seams.

3) Slip one leg inside the other, right sides together. Stitch crotch seam on pants, using a reinforcing stretch stitch or double-stitched narrow seam. Zigzag or overedge upper edge of pants.

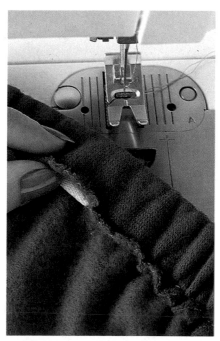

4) Form casing by folding over waist edge an amount equal to width of elastic plus ½" (1.3 cm). Stitch casing so distance between fold and stitches equals width of elastic plus ⅛" (3 mm). Leave 2" (5 cm) opening to insert elastic.

5) Thread elastic through casing, using safety pin or bodkin. Lap ends of elastic ½" (1.3 cm), and stitch securely with closely spaced zigzag stitch.

6) Slip lapped seam of elastic into opening in casing. Stitch opening closed, stretching elastic as you sew. Finish leg edges with ribbing, hem, or elastic in casing (page 66).

How to Sew a Ribbing Waistband with Drawstring

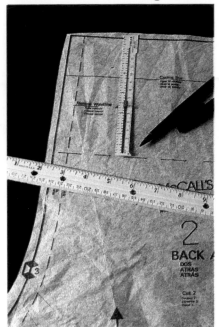  

1) Mark cutting line on pattern below waistline a distance equal to the finished depth of ribbing, minus ¼" (6 mm) seam allowance. Mark cutting line 2¼" (5.7 cm) below waistline for 2½" (6.5 cm) ribbing waistband.

2) Cut ribbing 5½" (14 cm) deep (twice finished depth plus seam allowances). Cut ribbing to equal two-thirds measurement at cut edge of waistline; add ½" (1.3 cm) for seam allowances. Stitch ribbing ends in ¼" (6 mm) seam, and finger press seam open.

3) Fold ribbing in half lengthwise. Lightly press fold. Insert grommet or make small buttonhole through single layer of ribbing at center front, below fold. Grommet or buttonhole will be used for drawstring insertion.

How to Sew a Ribbing Waistband with Elastic

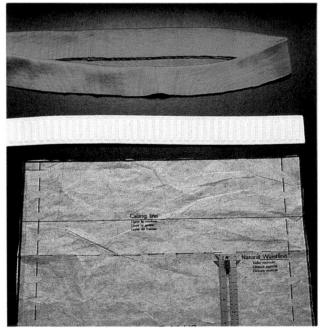 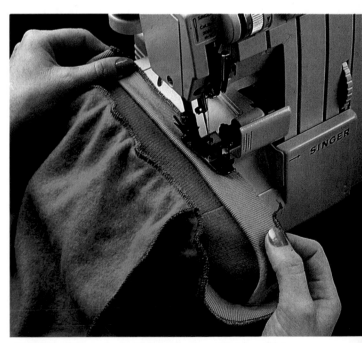

1) Mark cutting line on pattern ¼" (6 mm) above waistline. Cut ribbing twice the width of elastic, plus ½" (1.3 cm) for seam allowances. Determine length of ribbing and stitch as in step 2, above.

2) Fold ribbing in half lengthwise. Divide ribbing and waist edge into fourths with pins. With raw edges even, pin ribbing to right side of pants. Stitch; stretch ribbing as you sew. Leave 2" (5 cm) opening in seam for elastic insertion.

  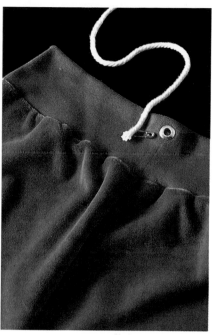

4) Divide ribbing and waist edge into fourths, and mark with pins. For larger waist, divide ribbing and garment into eighths.

5) Pin ribbing to pants, right sides together, matching markers and placing grommet opening or buttonhole at center front on right side of pants. Stitch, using straight stitch, narrow zigzag, or overlock; stretch ribbing as you sew.

6) Insert drawstring with bodkin or safety pin. To reinforce, topstitch ribbing seam. If using twin needle, straddle seam so one line of topstitching falls on each side of seam.

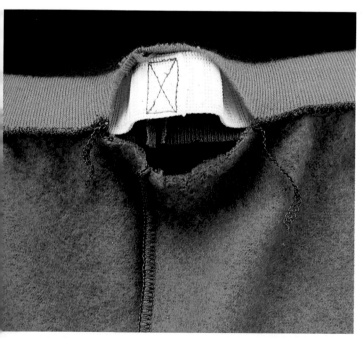 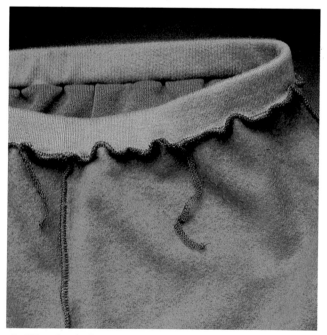

3) Cut elastic long enough to fit waist comfortably, plus ½" (1.3 cm) for overlap. Insert elastic through opening in ribbing seam. Lap ends of elastic, and stitch securely.

4) Slip elastic into seam opening in ribbing. To finish, stitch opening edges of waistband together.

How to Sew a Casing of Elastic with a Built-in Drawstring

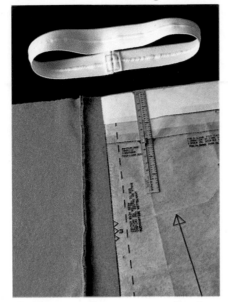

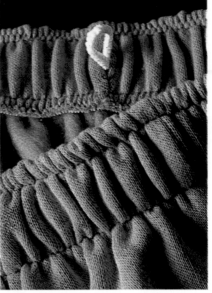

1) Cut pants from pattern, allowing 3" (7.5 cm) above waistline for casing. Cut elastic 2" (5 cm) shorter than waist measurement. Join ends of elastic in ½" (1.3 cm) seam. Open seam, and stitch rectangle through seam allowances and elastic.

2) Leave seam open ½" (1.3 cm) at center front in drawstring area. Topstitch around seam opening. Divide elastic into fourths, and pin to pants with edges even, placing elastic seam at center back. Zigzag both edges of elastic to pants, stretching elastic as you sew.

3) Fold elastic to inside on inner edge of elastic. Stitch ¼" (6 mm) from upper and lower edge of casing, stretching elastic as you sew. Pull drawstring through center front opening to inside of garment. Cut drawstring, and knot ends.

How to Sew a Casing with Multiple Rows of Elastic

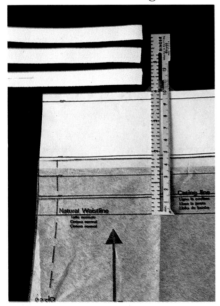

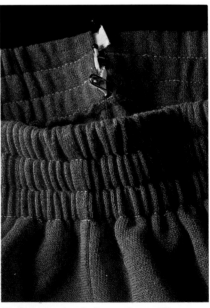

1) Mark casing on pattern, above waistline. Allow ⅝" (1.5 cm) for each row of ½" (1.3 cm) elastic; then double the amount, and add ¼" (6 cm) seam allowance. Allow 4" (10 cm) for waist finish shown. Cut elastic to fit waist comfortably, plus ½" (1.3 cm) overlap.

2) Stitch pants seams, leaving center back seam open at casing. Fold casing to wrong side, and press. Stitch parallel rows ⅝" (1.5 cm) apart, forming three equal casings for elastic.

3) Insert elastic in casings. Place straight pin at one end of elastic to prevent it from slipping into casing. Work all three elastics through casings at the same time. Lap ends of elastic, and stitch securely. Slip lapped seams back into casings. Slipstitch to close.

How to Sew an Elasticized Waistline (stitched-on method)

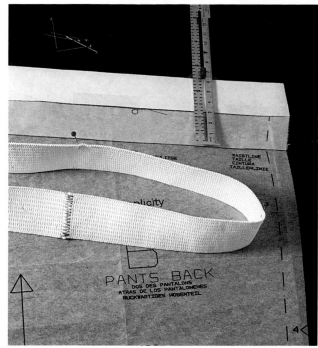

1) Mark cutting line for casing on pants front and back pattern above waist symbol. Casing allowance equals twice the width of elastic used. Cut elastic to length that fits snugly around hips. Butt ends of elastic, and join them with zigzag stitches. Divide elastic into fourths, and mark with pins.

2) Pin elastic to wrong side of casing so that edge of elastic and raw edge of casing match, placing one pin marker at each pants seam. Serge or zigzag elastic to casing, stretching elastic to fit. On overlock machine, disengage cutting blades, or guide work carefully to avoid cutting into elastic.

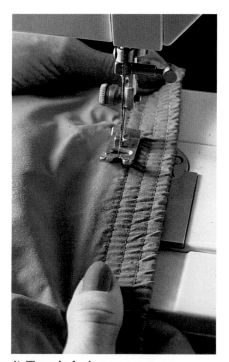

3) Fold elastic to wrong side of pants so casing covers elastic. From right side of pants, stitch in the ditch of all four pants seams to anchor elastic for easier handling.

4) Topstitch three or more rows through all layers of casing, stretching elastic as you sew. Use long stitch. Space rows evenly ¼" (6 mm) apart by using width of presser foot as stitching guide.

Alternative method. Stitch next to lower edge of casing inside pants, stretching elastic as you sew and using long stitch. Stitch again ¼" (6 mm) above first row of stitching, stretching elastic as you sew.

Leg Finishes

The leg finishes for sweatpants or warm-ups can comfortably hug the ankle or hang freely.

Casing with elastic provides an easy-to-sew fitted leg finish.

Ribbing leg finish is snug at the ankle. To add ribbing, cut the pants at the finished length as given on the pattern. The depth of the ribbing adds necessary ease to the length of the pants.

Hem that is topstitched is the fastest finish for a leg opening that hangs freely and does not fit close to the ankle; hemmed pants are easy to remove over tennis or running shoes.

Zipper on the lower pants leg provides an alternative. The pants are easy to take off over tennis or running shoes, yet can be snug at the ankle for cold-weather activities. Use a lightweight synthetic coil zipper for a smooth, nonbulky opening. Insert the zipper to extend from the knee to the lower edge of the pants, using either the centered or lapped application.

Three Ways to Finish Leg Openings

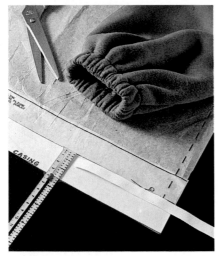

Casing. To add the casing length, allow for twice the width of the elastic, plus ½" (1.3 cm). Cut the elastic to fit comfortably around the ankle, plus ½" (1.3 cm) seam allowances. To stitch, follow the method for a waistline (page 61).

Ribbing. Cut ribbing 6½" (16.3 cm) deep and length required to fit comfortably around ankle, plus ½" (1.3 cm) seam allowances. Attach ribbing by flat or tubular method (page 55).

Hem. Mark cutting line, allowing 1¼" (3.2 cm) for hem. After turning hem up, stitch ¾" (2 cm) from fold with twin needle. Trim hem allowance close to stitching.

How to Sew a Zippered Leg Opening

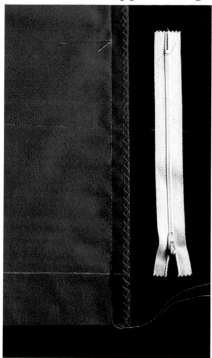

1) Stitch leg outseam; above pants hemline, leave opening equal to length of zipper. Machine-baste opening closed. Press seam open; finish raw edges. Stitch inseam after zipper is finished.

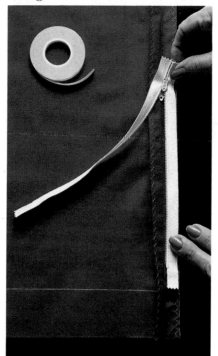

2) Open zipper. Place coil, face down, next to basted seam on back seam allowance of pants leg, right side of zipper facing wrong side of pants leg. Baste zipper in place with glue stick or basting tape.

3) Machine-baste next to teeth, using zipper foot. Stitch through zipper tape and seam allowance only. Close zipper.

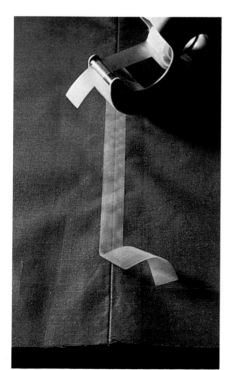

4) Mark stitching guide on right side of pants with strip of ½" (1.3 cm) wide tape applied over basted opening.

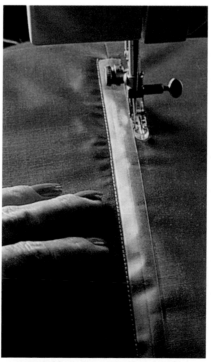

5) Stitch around edge of tape, using zipper foot. Remove tape and basting stitches.

6) Hem pants with machine stitching, angling ends of hem allowance away from edge.

Casings & Cuffs

Sleeves on sweatshirts, pullovers, and jackets can be finished with elasticized casings or ribbed cuffs. With both methods, the sleeve openings draw snugly around the wrists, then stretch to fit over mittens or gloves. For long wear, use heavy nylon/spandex ribbing for jacket cuffs. If you have chosen a ribbing waistband for the jacket, cut sleeve cuffs from matching ribbing for a professional look.

How to Sew an Elasticized Casing

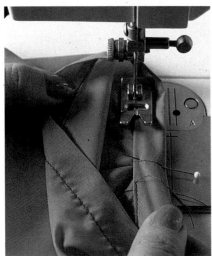

1) Turn under raw edge ¼" (6 mm), and press. Turn under casing on foldline, and press. Edgestitch close to fold at upper edge of casing, leaving an opening to insert elastic.

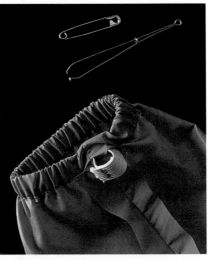

2) Cut elastic to fit the wrist comfortably, plus ¼" (6 mm) for seam allowances. Elastic should be ⅛" (3 mm) narrower than casing. Insert elastic into casing with safety pin or bodkin. Overlap ends ¼" (6 mm); stitch securely.

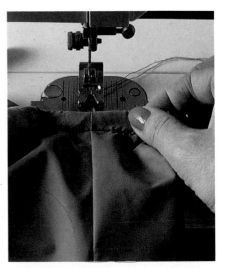

3) Slip joined ends of elastic into casing. Stitch opening in casing. To prevent the elastic from twisting, stitch in the ditch of sleeve seam through all layers of the casing.

How to Sew a Ribbing Cuff

1) Cut cuffs from ribbing. Depth of ribbing equals twice the finished width of cuffs plus ½" (1.3 cm) for seam allowances. Cutting guide on page 54 suggests depth for sleeve cuffs. Length of ribbing equals two-thirds the measurement around sleeve opening.

2) Stitch ends of ribbing together in ¼" (6 mm) seam. Fold cuff in half lengthwise, wrong sides together. Divide cuff into halves, and mark with pins, placing one pin at seams.

3) Trim seams on sleeve edge to ¼" (6 mm). Divide edge into halves, and mark with pins, placing one pin at seam. Pin cuff to right side of sleeve, matching pins.

4) Serge or zigzag-stitch ¼" (6 mm) seam. Stretch cuff to fit as you sew. Press seam toward garment.

Shirts & Shorts

Knit shirts and easy-fitting shorts can include features that are not only comfortable but also functional for either sports or leisure activities. Practical details such as pockets, bindings, and reinforcements are easily added to a basic pattern, so a variety of fashion details are possible with one pattern. On basic shirts and shorts, use elasticized waistbands, ribbed edges, or other comfort details traditionally found on sweatsuits and warm-ups.

Shirts. Use time-saving techniques to finish edges on T-shirts, tank tops, and similar pullover knit tops. Stitch hems by machine with a stretch blind hem stitch or twin-needle topstitching. On a three-thread overlock machine, serge blind hems for a finish like that on ready-to-wear shirts. Use a mock-cuff hem (page 41) for a cuffed look on sleeves and edges.

Narrow binding, cut from self-fabric or a contrasting fabric, is an alternative edge finish that looks like a trim. Apply binding to neckline, sleeves, armholes, or lower edges. Cut the binding crosswise on a lightweight knit. Polyester fold-over tape (page 122) can also be used to finish edges of sweatshirt fleece.

Modify the traditional rugby shirt by making it from lightweight single knit or an easy-care polyester blend.

Shorts. Comfort is an essential feature of shorts for running, tennis, golf, and other exercise activities. Patterns can be modified to suit the athletic event. Running shorts, for example, usually have a split-leg finish for full movement. The binding technique used on T-shirts and tank tops can also be used on fitness shorts.

Camp shorts are longer and fuller in the leg than fitness shorts. A double seat/back pocket makes camp shorts strong and durable. Use a rugged twill fabric for these shorts. Pocket design is also an important feature on other styles of shorts. No matter what the design of the pocket, it should be useful and convenient.

To eliminate bulk on side seam pockets, especially in sweatshirt fleece, finish the edge with a reinforcing twill tape instead of a facing. This technique is also used on sweatshirts and pullover tops to eliminate a double layer of bulky fabric on the curved edge of a pouch or kangaroo pocket. To secure contents in patch pockets, use a heavy-duty snap or a circle of hook and loop tape at the upper edge of the pocket.

Binding Edges

To finish leg openings on split-leg shorts or to finish necklines, sleeves, armholes, and lower edges on T-shirts and tank tops, use a knit binding. A binding of soft, lightweight knit or ribbing shapes easily to the curved leg, neck, or arm opening and feels comfortable against your skin.

For split-leg shorts, cut the binding as long as the leg opening from the side seam in the back at the leg opening, around the lower edge, to the side seam in front at the waist. Finish the waist of shorts using one of the methods given for sweatpants and warm-ups on pages 60 to 65. The waist finish shown is stitched elastic (page 65).

For T-shirts and tank tops, the length of the binding equals the measurement of the garment edge, plus 2" (5 cm) for finishing the ends. Trim the garment seam allowance on the seamline.

Cutting. Cut binding so greater stretch runs along its length. Cut it four times the finished width. Binding shown is cut 1" (2.5 cm) wide for finished width of ¼" (6 mm).

How to Apply Binding to Split-leg Shorts

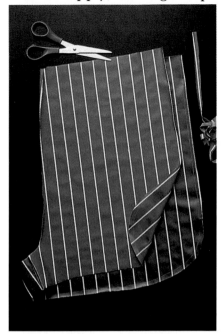

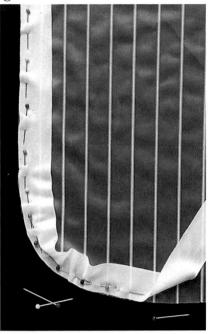

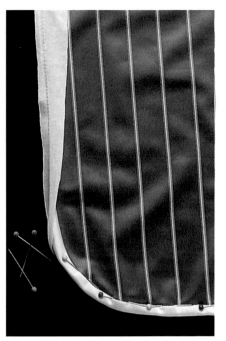

1) Stitch inseam of each shorts leg. Mark side seamline on back of shorts. To adapt a pattern for this finish, trim seam and hem allowances to ¼" (6 mm).

2) Pin binding to leg opening, right sides together, beginning at side seam in back. Continue around leg opening and up side seam in front to waist edge. Ease binding around curves. Stitch ¼" (6 mm) from cut edge.

3) Fold binding down to press seam. Wrap binding over seam allowances to wrong side, encasing seam allowance.

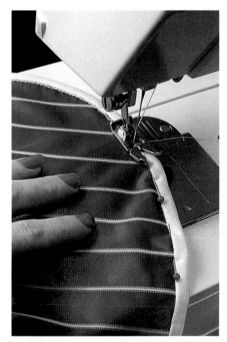

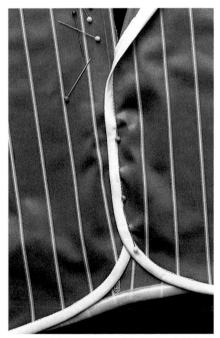

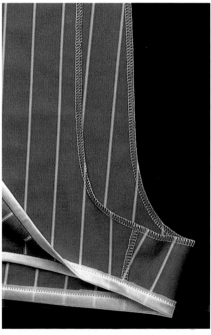

4) Stitch in the ditch of the binding seam, stitching from the right side. This stitching secures binding on wrong side of leg opening. Press lightly.

5) Lap bound front side seam over back raw edge, matching stitching line with side seamline marking. Pin. Starting at leg opening, secure stitching and stitch in the ditch of the binding seam; stitch through all layers up to waist seamline.

6) Slip one leg inside the other, right sides together. Pin and stitch crotch seam of shorts in continuous seam from front to back. Serge, reinforce with two rows of stitching, or use reinforcement knit stitch.

How to Finish Edges with Knit Binding

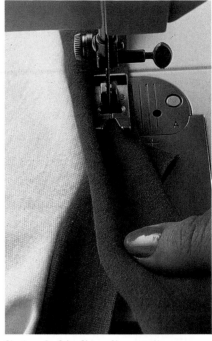

1) Stitch binding to garment edge with right sides together. Seam allowance equals finished width of binding. Stretch binding slightly as you sew so finished binding hugs the body.

2) Stop stitching exactly at the beginning of the binding. Leave needle in seam, and raise presser foot; fold the beginning of binding away from garment.

3) Angle binding diagonally away from garment. Continue stitching to join binding, stretching upper layer of binding slightly. Stop stitching at the edge of the under binding layer.

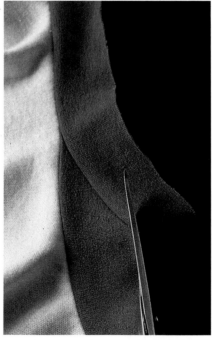

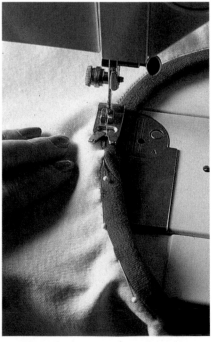

4) Trim the under layer of binding even with raw edge of upper layer.

5) Fold upper layer of binding away from garment. Trim excess binding to make binding uniform width. Press lightly.

6) Fold binding over seam allowances to wrong side. Pin just past seamline. Binding must be taut and smooth. From the right side, stitch in the ditch of the seam. On inside, trim ⅛" (3 mm) from stitching.

Twill-tape Rugby Placket

Authentic rugby shirts are traditionally strong, long-wearing sports uniforms made from heavy cotton knit. Collars are rib knit or woven cotton twill reinforced with twill tape at the neckline seam. The front placket opening is faced with twill tape, and buttons are concealed with a twill-tape flap.

Marking. Although the buttons and buttonholes line up on the center front of the shirt, the actual placket opening is off-center. Mark the center front; mark the placket opening half the width of the twill tape. For men's shirts, mark the opening on the right-hand side of the center front so the finished placket laps left over right. For women's shirts, mark on the left-hand side so the lap is in the opposite direction. Mark the finished length of the placket.

How to Sew a Twill-tape Rugby Placket

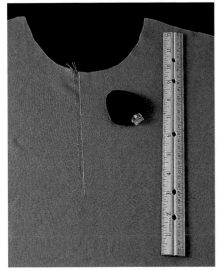

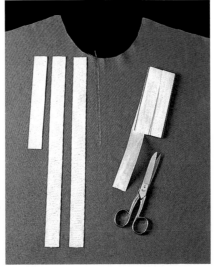

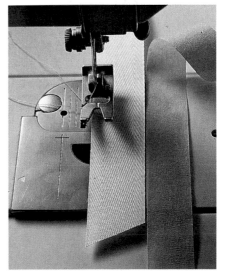

1) Mark placket position to one side of center front. Staystitch placket opening; shorten stitches at point, and take one short stitch across point. Slash through center of staystitching to point.

2) Cut three strips of twill tape for the placket: cut two strips twice the finished length of placket; cut one strip the length of placket.

3) Lay left-hand edge of twill tape under the machine needle. Place a strip of masking tape along the right-hand side of twill tape to use as a stitching guide.

(Continued on next page.)

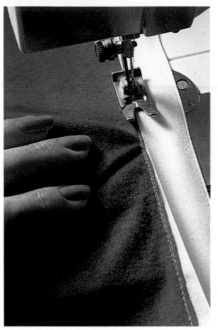

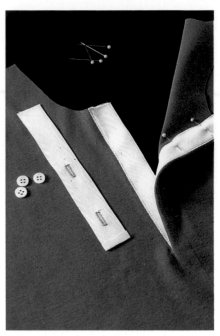

4) Lay placket opening, right side up, over one of the long strips of twill tape with staystitching line just overlapping the left-hand edge of twill tape. Stitch shirt to tape, following staystitching line and keeping right-hand edge of twill tape even with mark.

5) Lay the second long strip of twill tape over the first with edges even. Edgestitch the outer edge of tapes, then the inner edge, sandwiching the shirt between.

6) Fold the shirt overlap to the inside along the stitched inner edge of tape. Turn under ¼" (6 mm) on one end of the short strip of twill tape. Make buttonholes on tape.

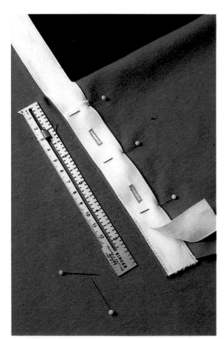

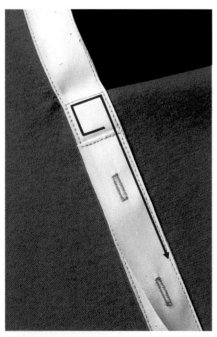

7) Pin short strip of twill tape on inside of placket overlap with finished end 1" (2.5 cm) above bottom of placket.

8) Edgestitch placket from the inside, starting at inner edge of tapes. Stitch in direction of arrows, across bottom of tape to bottom of placket, across bottom of placket and length of placket to neck edge.

9) Trim tapes evenly at neckline. Attach buttons to the underlap of tape. Make and attach collar (opposite).

How to Sew a Rugby Collar with Twill Tape

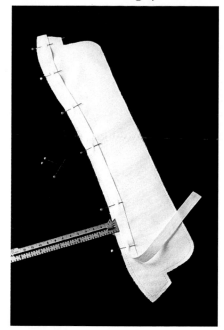

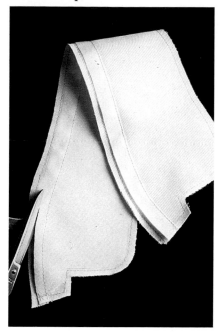

1) Pin ½" (1.3 cm) twill tape on right side of interfaced upper collar, lining up lower edge of tape on neck seamline of collar section. Stitch upper edge of tape to collar.

2) Trim upper collar ¼" (6 mm) from stitching. Work from wrong side of collar section to trim; do not cut through twill tape.

3) Stitch collar sections, right sides together. Neck seamline of upper collar is at lower edge of tape. Raw edge and tape edge are not even. Trim and clip seam allowances, and turn right side out; press.

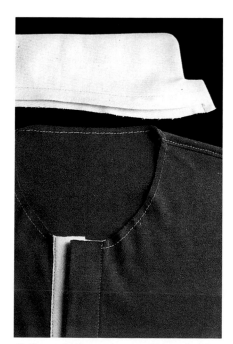

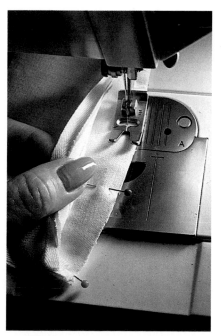

4) Staystitch neck seamline of shirt to prepare for collar application. Shirt shoulder seams have been pressed toward back of shirt and topstitched to prevent stretching.

5) Stitch undercollar to shirt with right sides together, folding upper collar out of the way so it is not caught in this seam. Press seam allowance toward collar.

6) Pin taped edge of upper collar over neckline seam so lower edge of tape covers stitching. Stitch edge of tape through all layers. Continue edgestitching around collar.

Pockets

On sportswear, pockets are functional and often decorative. If you are adding pockets to a pattern, carefully consider placement; to be useful, the pockets must be within easy reach. They should also be a size that is appropriate to their use.

Patch pocket is easy to add to a garment even if the pattern does not include it. Cut a patch pocket from self-fabric, hem it along one edge, press under the raw edges, and sew the pocket to the garment. A machine application is appropriate for all sportswear. Two rows of machine stitching make patch pockets more durable.

Pouch pocket is a special patch pocket that has an opening on each side. Stitched onto the front of a garment, it is large enough to keep both hands warm or to keep items such as maps and compass handy. Taped edges are especially suitable for knits.

They hide all the seam allowances, eliminate bulk, and stay the pocket openings so they will not stretch.

Lapped side pocket can be added to pants and shorts if the pattern does not include a pocket pattern piece. With this method, the shorts or pants front pattern is a cutting guide for the pocket. To make the pocket strong and prevent the pocket opening from stretching, face the opening with twill tape. Topstitching on the completed lapped pocket blends into the topstitching on the seams for a professional finish.

Combination double seat/patch pocket uses the back pattern piece of shorts or pants as a cutting guide. Reinforcing with a double layer of fabric makes the garment more durable for activities such as camping, mountain climbing, and hiking. Secure the pocket opening with a circle of hook and loop tape.

How to Apply a Patch Pocket

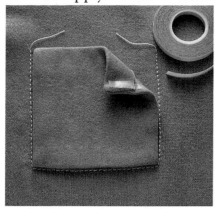

1) Mark pocket placement line with machine basting to provide clear guideline for positioning pocket. Use basting tape, pins, or glue stick to hold pocket in place on right side of garment.

2) Edgestitch pocket to garment. Add a second row of topstitching to increase durability or to match topstitched seams used elsewhere on garment.

3) Pull threads to inside, and tie to secure. Add a decorative snap or hook and loop closure. Remove machine basting.

How to Sew a Taped Pouch Pocket

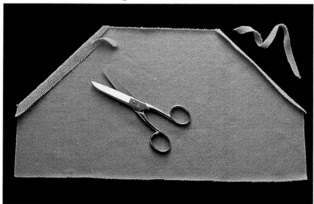

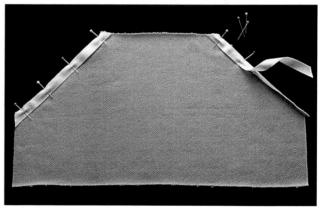

1) Turn seam allowances under on both pocket opening edges. Press. Trim seam allowances to ¼" (6 mm).

2) Pin ½" (1.3 cm) wide twill tape next to edge of openings on wrong side of pocket, covering raw edges. For curved openings, steam press tape to match shape before pinning.

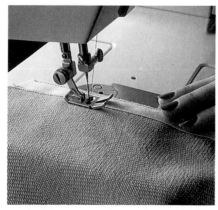

3) Edgestitch both edges of tape to pocket. Keep pocket flat as you sew. Press.

4) Turn seam allowances under at sides and top of pocket. Press. Pin pocket to garment.

5) Edgestitch top and sides; then topstitch to match stitching on tape. Finish bottom of pocket in hem or ribbing.

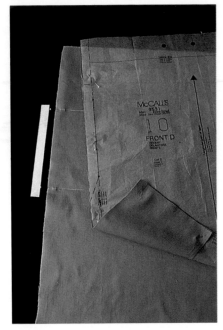

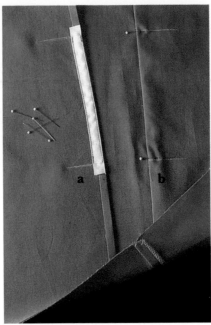

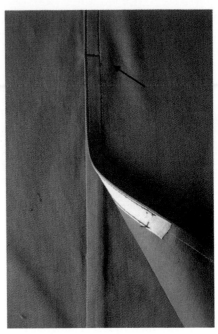

1) Cut pocket, using pattern front as guide. Cut pocket as long as shorts front from waist to hem, and 5" to 6" (12.5 to 15 cm) wide. Cut ½" (1.3 cm) wide twill tape 1" (2.5 cm) longer than the pocket opening.

2) Press side seam allowance on front to wrong side. Trim to ¼" (6 mm). Pin twill tape over pocket opening next to fold, covering raw edge. Stitch close to both edges of tape **(a)**. Stitch pocket section to back at side. Finish seam, and press toward pocket **(b)**.

3) Lap front over back at side seam, with taped edge even with seamline. Edgestitch seam at top and bottom of pocket opening. Topstitch seam again to match stitching. Make a bar tack at each end of pocket opening (arrow).

4) Finish inside edge of pocket. Pin and stitch to front. Include raw edge at top of pocket in stitching for waistline finish.

5) Finish shorts or pants by stitching crotch seam, attaching elastic, and finishing waistband, using techniques on pages 62 to 65. Hem; include lower edge of pocket in stitching for leg opening finish.

How to Add a Combination Double Seat/Patch Pocket

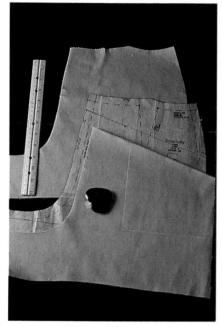 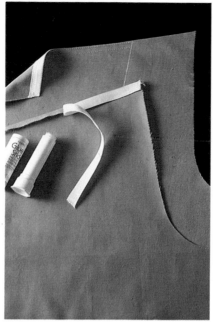 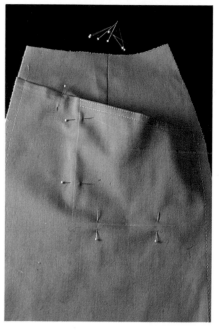

1) Use shorts back pattern to make seat/pocket. Slant upper cutting line from 1" (2.5 cm) below waist at center back to 4" (10 cm) below waist at side seam. Mark pocket opening on upper cutting line 6" (15 cm) from side seam. Mark bottom of pocket at midpoint on side seam. Use shorts cutting line at hem for seat.

2) Press under upper raw edge of seat ¼" (6 mm). Baste ½" (1.3 cm) wide twill tape over raw edge on wrong side. Edgestitch tape at pocket opening; then topstitch ¼" (6 mm) from edgestitching.

3) Pin one seat to each shorts back section at raw edges and pocket stitching line. Machine-baste shorts and seat together at crotch seam, inseam, and side seam.

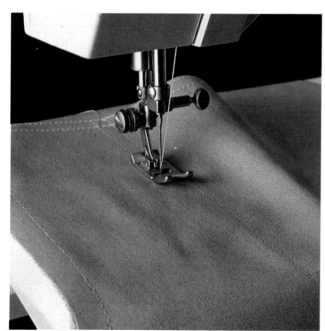 

4) Edgestitch seat to shorts along upper edge, stopping at pocket opening. Topstitch ¼" (6 mm) away. Stitch two rows ¼" (6 mm) apart to form pocket, stitching straight down from upper edge, then across to side seam.

5) Add circle of hook and loop tape to pocket opening if desired. Complete shorts, following pattern directions.

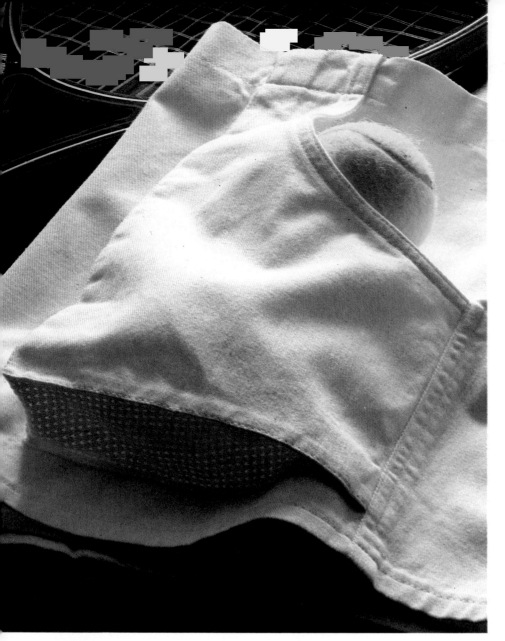

Expandable Pockets

Add a gusset, or shaped insert, to a patch pocket so the pocket can expand to hold extra tennis or golf balls. As you empty the pocket during a game, the gusset folds up so the pocket lies flat. Cut gussets from knitted mesh or contrasting fabric for a contrast in color or texture, or cut them in one with the pocket.

How to Make an Expandable Pocket

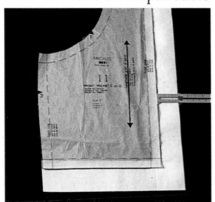

1) **Adapt** pocket pattern by adding 2" (5 cm) from seamline at lower and inner side edges. Pattern extensions form expandable gusset in completed pocket.

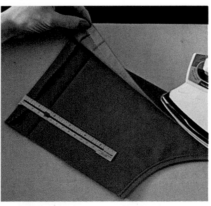

2) **Finish** pocket according to pattern directions. Press under ½" (1.3 cm) seam allowance on raw edges. Fold gusset under 1½" (3.8 cm), and press.

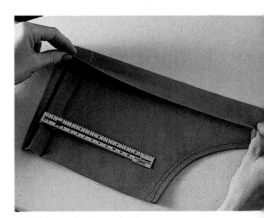

3) **Bring** the two folded edges of gusset together to form a ¾" (2 cm) pleat on side and lower edge. Press.

How to Make an Expandable Patch Pocket with Mesh Gusset

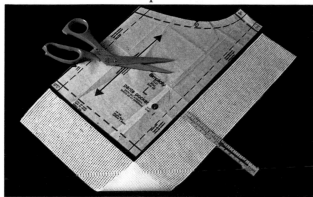

1) **Cut** 3" (7.5 cm) wide mesh gusset as long as combined length and width measurement of pocket edges. Greatest amount of stretch should be crosswise on strip. Finish pocket opening according to pattern directions.

2) **Stitch** gusset to inner side edge of pocket, right sides together, in ⅝" (1.5 cm) seam. Hold gusset taut, but do not stretch it. With needle in fabric, stop stitching ⅝" (1.5 cm) from corner.

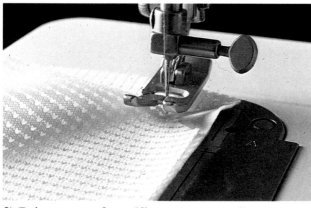

3) **Raise** presser foot. Clip gusset seam allowance at corner of pocket. Pivot. Lower presser foot, and pull gusset taut to stitch remainder of seam.

4) **Trim** excess fabric at corner. Press seam toward gusset. Turn to right side. Press under seam allowance on raw edge of gusset. Trim seam to ¼" (6 mm). To apply pocket, follow step 6, below.

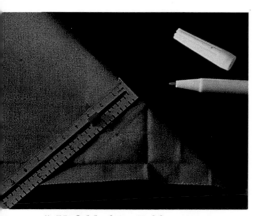

4) **Unfold** pleat. Fold gusset corner diagonally, right sides together. Mark stitching line for miter in shape of a reversed Z. Inner point of Z is on pleat fold 1" (2.5 cm) from diagonal fold of corner.

5) **Stitch** miter on marked line, using short stitches. Trim seam to ¼" (6 mm). Clip to stitches at point of miter. Finger press seam open. Turn to right side; press.

6) **Edgestitch** upper fold of gusset. Pin pocket to garment, keeping edgestitched fold of gusset out of the way. Edgestitch pocket to garment. Machine-baste pocket to waistline and side seam of shorts.

Outerwear

Sewing Outerwear

Outerwear garments offer protection from cold, wind, rain, or snow. For active sports, such as golf, running, cross-country skiing, and sailing, one of the most versatile garments is the *shell*. A shell is an unlined jacket or pullover top with a loose fit so it can be worn over other garments as a protective cover. Outerwear shells are usually sewn from fabrics that are windproof and either waterproof or water repellent. Additional features for retaining body heat are hoods and body-hugging cuffs and lower edges.

Basic shell. A jacket shell has a center front zipper and set-in or raglan sleeves. Many adaptations are possible with this versatile garment, shown opposite. For example, a shell with a wind shield across the back and a self-storing hood offers increased protection from bad weather; for safety at night, trim the shell with reflective tape.

Ventilating wind shield. For comfort, a garment made from a coated waterproof fabric needs either to fit loosely enough so body heat can evaporate or to have grommets or mesh inserts for ventilation. To add this comfort feature to a basic shell, split the back pattern piece into two sections and add an overlapping back panel for extra protection from wind and rain. Underneath the panel, insert a layer of athletic mesh for ventilation.

Self-storing hood. A collar on a jacket, windbreaker, or poncho can conveniently store a drawstring hood. The hood folds into the collar when not in use, and a strip of hook and loop tape keeps it neatly secured at center back. A lightweight fabric is the best choice for this detail. If the body of the garment is made of quilted or insulated fabric, use lining fabric for the hood and it will fold compactly without adding unwanted weight or bulk to the garment neckline.

Waist and sleeve finishes. Choose from several alternatives for the finish at the waistline and sleeve edges. The waistline may be finished with one or more rows of elastic in a single casing or with a drawstring. For reinforcement on a ribbed waistband, use self-fabric between the ribbing and the zipper.

Zippers. Exposed separating sports zippers are practical and attractive for outerwear garments. For pullover shells or powder jackets, lightweight coil zippers can be used.

Pockets. Pockets also offer choices in design features. Zippered pockets secure contents and protect against lost articles — especially important on garments worn for active sports. A pocket can even be used to create a storage pouch for a pullover top or rain poncho. Add an elastic belt to the inside of the pocket, and the pouch with poncho or pullover tucked inside can be worn around your waist when the weather is warm and clear.

Polyester fleece. Many of the sewing techniques used for making an unlined shell can be used for sewing a warm jacket or pullover top from polyester fleece. A fleece jacket does not require lining. Edges can be finished with fold-over braid or a lightweight strip of stretch binding.

Self-storing rain poncho. A waterproof poncho is a simple but practical garment that can be made with a garment-storing pocket for convenience. Keep the poncho at hand in a purse, backpack, or glove compartment until it is needed.

Insulated outerwear. Insulated jackets, vests, or pants add extra protection in colder weather. They are made from an outer layer of waterproof or water repellent fabric and an inner layer of insulating material. Customize the garment to suit weather conditions by choosing appropriate fabrics for the outer and insulating layers (pages 12 to 15).

Fabric Preparation

Preshrinking is not necessary for fabrics made from nylon fibers or nylon blends, coated fabrics, and fabrics with stain and water repellent chemical finishes. These fabrics will not shrink noticeably. Press out wrinkles before pattern layout; use a low heat setting on the iron to prevent heat damage to nylon or coated fabrics. Lightly press seams open using a low iron temperature, or finger press.

How to Add a Back Wind Shield and Reflective Tape

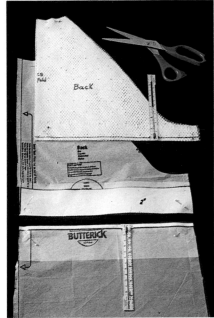

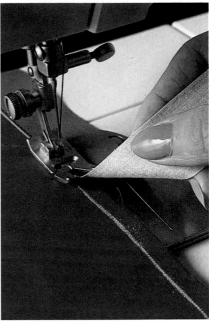

1) Cut jacket back pattern 1" (2.5 cm) below armhole to divide into two sections. To cut mesh insert, add ¼" (6 mm) seam allowance to upper section; add 2" (5 cm) overlap allowance to upper section to cut wind shield from jacket fabric. Add ¼" (6 mm) seam allowance to lower section.

2) Stitch mesh insert to lower jacket back in ¼" (6 mm) seam, right sides together. Finish raw edges by serging or zigzag-stitching them together, unless jacket fabric is uncoated nylon. Nylon fabric should be seared after cutting, as on page 23.

3) Lap reflective tape ¼" (6 mm) over lower edge of wind shield, with tape right side up on wrong side of wind shield. Edgestitch tape to wind shield.

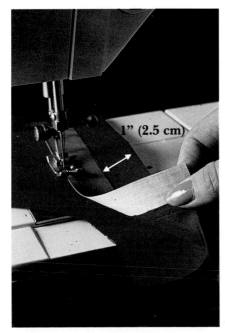

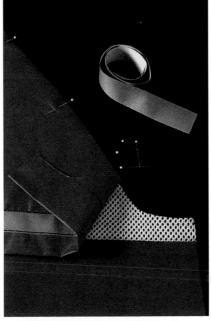

4) Fold tape to right side of wind shield, so 1" (2.5 cm) of fabric shows along lower edge. Press with iron at low heat setting. Stitch free edge of tape to wind shield.

5) Lay wind shield over mesh insert on upper jacket back, right side of both layers facing up. Machine-baste wind shield and jacket back together at neckline, armholes, and side seams.

6) Add tape to jacket front to line up with tape on wind shield; topstitch in place. Tape forms contrast stripe around finished jacket. Finish jacket according to pattern directions.

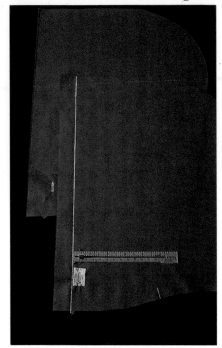

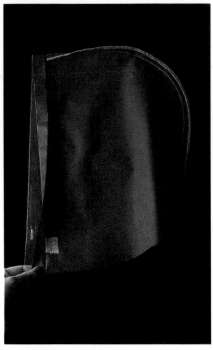

1) Make buttonholes for drawstring on each side of hood, 1" (2.5 cm) above neck seamline and ⅜" (1 cm) from casing foldline. On wrong side, reinforce buttonhole with interfacing.

2) Stitch center back seam of hood. Serge seam or use French seam so raw edges are finished. For drawstring casing, press under raw edge ¼" (6 mm). Turn under casing on foldline, and press.

3) Unfold pressed casing. Turn under double narrow hem on front neckline of hood. Taper hem into raw edge of back neckline slightly beyond shoulder seam marks. Edgestitch hem.

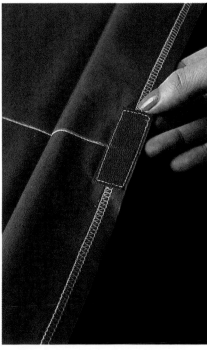

7) Prepare collar. Press center foldline of collar. Press seam allowance under on collar neckline. Finish one long edge of collar with serging, zigzag overcasting, or clean finishing.

8) Stitch hook portion of hook and loop tape to wrong side of collar at center back above neck seamline.

9) Pin unfinished edge of collar to neckline with right side of collar toward wrong side of garment. Stitch neck seam, including basted hood in stitching. Insert zipper (pages 94 and 95).

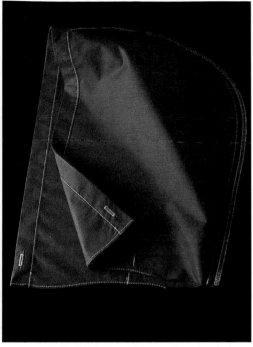

4) Fold drawstring casing back into pressed position. Stitch inner edge of casing.

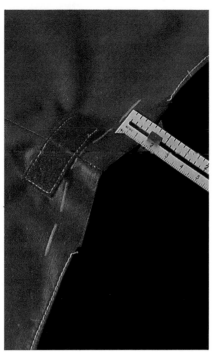

5) Stitch loop portion of 1" to 2" (2.5 to 5 cm) strip of hook and loop tape to center back of hood. Position tape above neck seamline on right side of hood.

6) Pin right side of hood to right side of garment on back neckline seam, between shoulder markings. Machine-baste hood to garment between shoulder marks.

10) Fold short ends of collar back on each other with right sides together, covering zipper tape. Stitch, following zipper stitching. Trim and grade seams.

11) Turn collar right side out. Pin pressed-under seam allowance at free edge of collar to neckline seam, covering stitching line. From right side, stitch from center front to shoulder seam; backstitch.

12) Repeat with other side of collar, leaving collar open between shoulder seams. Insert drawstring in casing. To store hood, roll up and insert in collar. Press hook and loop tape together.

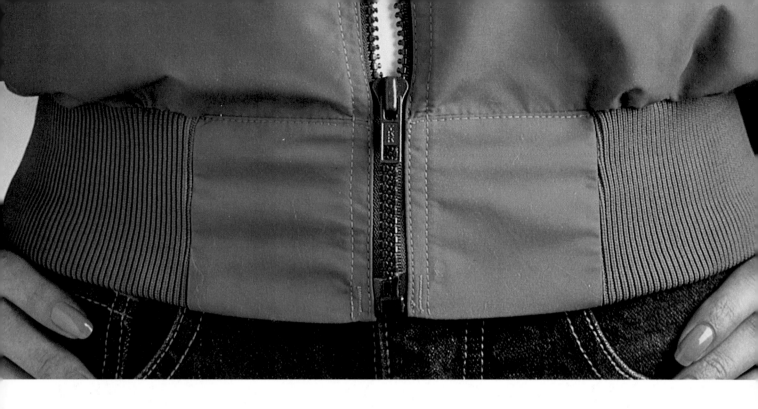

Jacket Waistbands

With most waist-length jackets you can easily adapt a zip-front pattern to use a casing or ribbing.

Casing waistband is easy and quick to sew. Use elastic or a drawstring in the casing.

Ribbing waistband of durable nylon or nylon/spandex rib knit is especially snug and comfortable. Tab inserts cut from the jacket fabric reinforce and finish the ends of the ribbing; the zipper is stitched to these tabs.

How to Sew a Casing Waistband

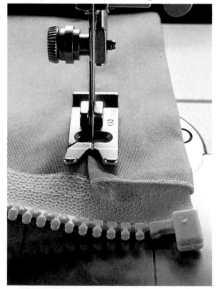 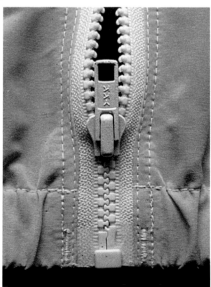 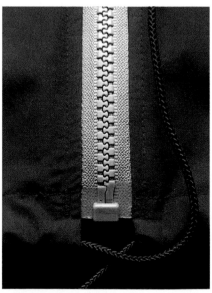

1) Apply separating zipper (pages 94 and 95). Press under ¼" (6 mm) on lower edge; press under casing on foldline. Edgestitch close to fold at upper edge of casing. Cut elastic to fit waist comfortably. Insert into casing. Machine-baste across casing and elastic.

2) Stitch across ends of elastic and casing as you topstitch zipper. Trim excess elastic close to topstitching. Make bar tacks at ends, stitching through elastic and zipper.

Alternative method. Apply zipper with bottom stop ½" (1.3 cm) above casing foldline. Insert drawstring. Knot ends, or thread through toggles to prevent from pulling out. Or stitch through drawstring at center back to prevent it from pulling out.

How to Sew a Ribbing Waistband

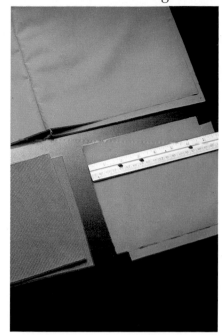

1) Cut ribbing twice finished depth plus ½" (1.3 cm) seam allowances, and 5" (12.5 cm) shorter than waist measurement. Cut two waistband tabs, each 7" (18 cm) wide and as long as cut depth of ribbing.

2) Fold tabs in half lengthwise, wrong sides together. Stitch short ends of ribbing to open ends of folded tabs in ¼" (6 cm) seam. Press tab seam allowance toward ribbing. Fold tabs in half, and mark center on right side.

3) Pin tabs to lower edge of jacket, lining up fold with front cut edge. Divide ribbing and jacket into fourths, and mark. Pin ribbing to jacket, matching markers. Stitch ¼" (6 mm) seam, stretching ribbing as you sew.

4) Apply separating zipper, page 94, steps 1 to 3. Fold tabs up to right side of jacket with folded edges even with front opening. At top of tab, fold under ¼" (6 mm). From right side, stitch over zipper stitching at front edge.

5) Turn tab and ribbing right side out. Clip seam allowance ¼" (6 mm) at tab/ribbing seams. From right side, stitch close to upper seam on tab to secure free edge.

6) Bring raw edges of ribbing together. Fold garment out of the way to overedge or serge ribbing edges together on previous stitching line. Press zipper to inside; topstitch as for separating zipper, page 95, step 6.

Exposed Separating Zipper

Separating zippers are used for convenient front closures on jackets, vests, and coats. For extra warmth, insert a separating zipper so it extends to the finished edge of a collar or neck ribbing. For a decorative accent on active sportswear, use a zipper of a contrasting color with large plastic teeth, inserted so the zipper teeth are exposed.

If you cannot find a separating zipper in the length needed, buy the next longer size and shorten it. Cut off excess length at the *top* of the zipper, allowing enough tape to fold the raw edge back at an angle. Stitch carefully between zipper teeth to secure fold.

The collar and lower edge of a jacket must be partially finished before the zipper is inserted, unless the lower edge is a casing; a casing is finished after the zipper is inserted. For a casing with a drawstring, position the bottom stop of the zipper ½" (1.3 cm) above the casing foldline.

How to Insert an Exposed Separating Zipper

1) Pin, glue, or use basting tape to baste one edge of closed zipper to garment, right sides together. Bottom stop of zipper is at hemline of garment. Top of zipper is at finished edge of collar.

2) Use zipper foot to stitch through center of zipper tape to allow for fabric thickness and width of slider. Fold excess tape at top of zipper, away from zipper teeth at an angle. Trim off excess zipper tape.

3) Fold zipper to wrong side of garment, exposing zipper. On free edge of zipper tape, mark location of details requiring matching. With right sides together, baste zipper to other side of garment, matching marks. Open zipper. Stitch free edge of zipper to garment.

Pullover tops with closely fitted collars or neck ribbings may require a zipper closure so the garment can be put on and taken off easily. These garments rarely have a seam where the zipper is needed, so an opening must be created with a stitching box, a rectangle of stitches sized to fit the zipper, slashed down the center, and finished with a facing. To insert a zipper in a pullover garment, use the instructions for a biking shirt (pages 48 and 49).

If you cannot find a zipper the correct length for a pullover garment, buy a zipper that is the next longer size, and shorten it from the *bottom*. Mark the desired length on the tape, above the zipper stop at the bottom. Make a new zipper stop by stitching several times across the tape at the mark, guiding the needle between the zipper teeth to avoid breaking or bending the needle. Cut off the excess zipper and tape below the new stop.

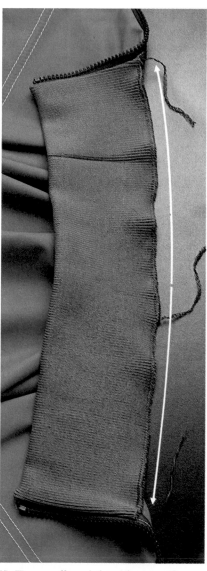

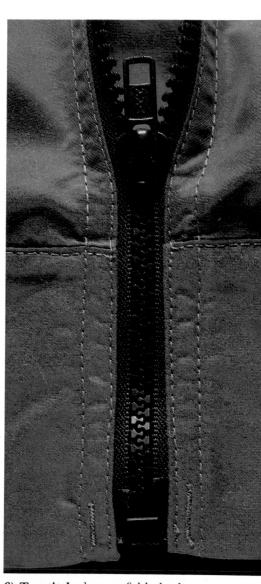

4) **Fold** ribbing or collar, right sides together, around and over zipper. Stitch on top of previous stitches, enclosing zipper in seam. Trim seam allowances across corner at collar fold.

5) **Turn** collar right side out. Pin or baste collar edge over neck seamline. Starting at center back (arrows), stitch ribbing to neckline seam, stretching ribbing as you sew. Serge or zigzag raw edge. Finish lower edge of jacket (pages 92 and 93).

6) **Topstitch** close to folded edge of fabric covering zipper. To reinforce, add second row of topstitching ¼" (6 mm) from edge. Reinforce bottom of zipper with bar tack.

Zippered Pockets

A pocket with a zippered opening keeps contents secure and seals out rain and snow. Zippered pockets can be sewn on shorts, pants, insulated jackets and vests, ponchos, and unlined shells. Position pockets according to pattern directions, or add pockets where you want them. Regardless of the shape and location of pockets or the slant of the zippered opening, the sewing method is the same.

Cut a pocket/self-lining section from the garment fabric, lining fabric, or outer shell fabric of insulated garments. To ventilate a waterproof garment when the pocket is zipped open, cut the pocket from fine athletic mesh. If the garment is for cold-weather wear, add a large zipper pull so you can open or close the pocket without removing gloves or mittens.

How to Sew a Zippered Pocket

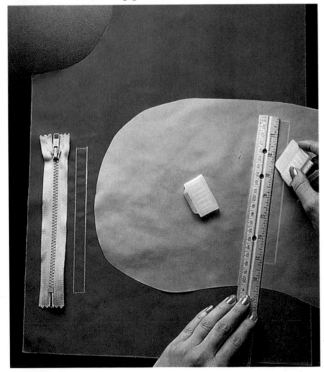

1) Mark stitching box for zipper opening with tailor's chalk on wrong side of pocket. Stitching box is the length of the zipper and wide enough to accommodate the zipper pull. Mark an identical stitching box on right side of the garment section.

2) Rub with scissor handle or edge of ruler to transfer marking from pocket to corresponding pocket for other side of garment. Transfer jacket marking the same way. This marking method ensures balanced zippered openings on garment.

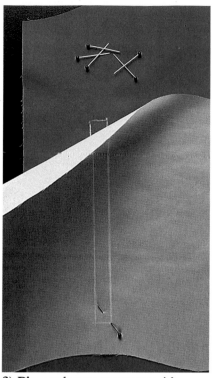

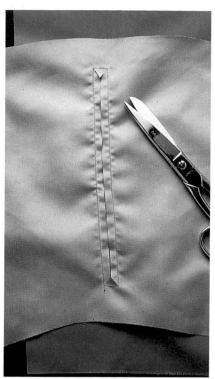

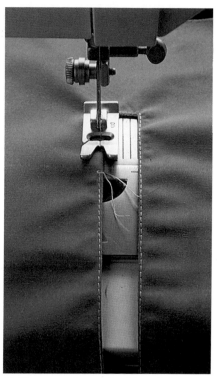

3) Pin pocket to garment with right sides together and stitching box markings matching.

4) Stitch around box, shortening stitches to pivot at corners and to stitch across ends. Cut through center of box, clipping diagonally to each corner.

5) Turn pocket to inside of the garment through cut opening. Edgestitch around the opening. Opening can also be understitched on pocket side.

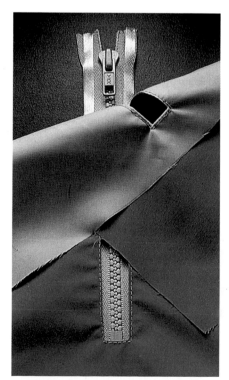

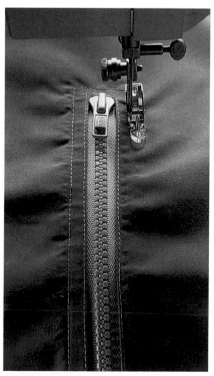

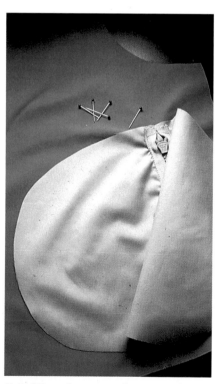

6) Baste zipper under opening with basting tape or glue stick, right sides of opening and zipper facing up.

7) Stitch scant ¼" (6 mm) from edgestitching, catching zipper tape in stitching.

8) Fold pocket over zipper, and pin sides of pocket together with raw edges even. Serge edges together, or stitch in ¼" (6 mm) seam and zigzag raw edges together.

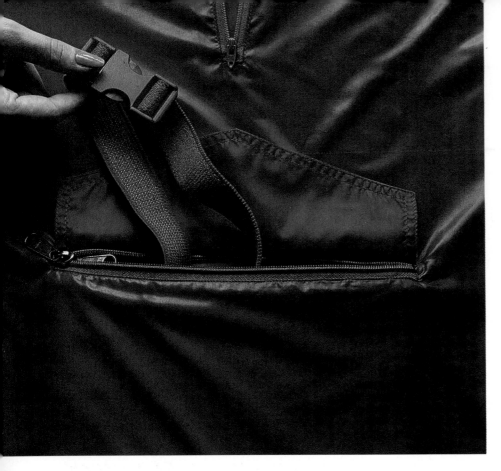

Garment-storing Pocket

Add a flapped pouch pocket to a lightweight pullover top to make the garment conveniently self-storing. Attach an elastic belt to the inside of the pocket. After folding the garment into the pocket, use the belt to wear the pouch around your waist.

Cutting. Cut one pocket piece 10" by 20" (25.5 by 51 cm), plus two 9½" by 4" (24.6 by 10 cm) pieces for the flap. For the closure, use a 9" (23 cm) reversible zipper, which has a pull on both sides. For the belt, use a lightweight ¾" (2 cm) plastic buckle and ¾" (2 cm) elastic approximately 10" (25.5 cm) shorter than your waist measurement.

How to Make a Garment-storing Pocket

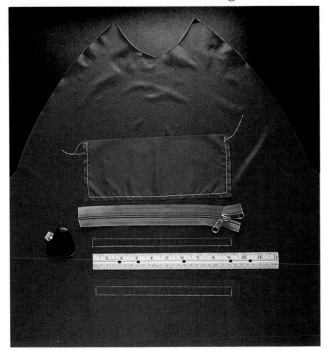

1) Mark 9" by ½" (23 by 1.3 cm) stitching guide for zipper opening on right side of garment about 3" (7.5 cm) below armholes. Mark similar stitching guide on wrong side of pocket piece, centered ½" (1.3 cm) below one short edge. Stitch flap sections, wrong sides together, around three sides in ¼" (6 mm) seam. Leave one long edge open. Trim across corners, and turn right side out. Topstitch.

2) Pin pocket to garment, right sides together, matching marked stitching guides. Starting on one long side, stitch on marking. Shorten stitches at corners and across short ends of rectangle for accuracy and reinforcement. Cut through center of rectangle; clip diagonally to each corner. Cut carefully. Do not cut into stitches.

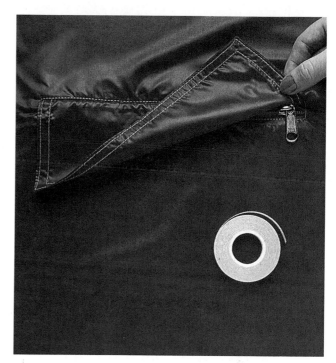

3) Turn pocket to wrong side through cut opening. Press lightly, rolling seams around opening to inside of garment. Use low heat setting. Machine-baste flap to right side of zipper on outer edge of tape.

4) Baste zipper to opening, with zipper and garment right side up. Topstitch zipper and flap to garment around opening. Make sure pocket underneath lies flat. Fold flap out of the way to stitch lower edge of zipper to garment.

5) Fold pocket up so raw edges of pocket meet above zipper opening. Fold garment out of the way, and stitch through flap, zipper tape, and upper edge of pocket. Cut elastic in half. Attach ends of elastic to buckle. With buckle closed to prevent elastic from twisting, slip free ends of elastic into pocket, just above fold. Pin.

6) Stitch sides of pocket in ¼" (6 mm) seam, catching ends of elastic in seam. Finish raw edges with serging or zigzag overcasting. Open zipper, and pull pocket out to store garment. Fold garment into pocket, close zipper, and buckle the belt around your waist.

Self-storing Rain Poncho

No pattern is needed to make a waterproof poncho with a cowl collar that can be worn as a hood. Use 3¼ yards (3.0 m) of 45" (115 cm) wide fabric or 2½ yards (2.3 m) of 60" (150 cm) wide fabric. Choose a lightweight coated nylon fabric soft enough to fold into the self-storing center pocket. You will also need a reversible zipper 9" (23 cm) long for the pocket closure. Use ¾" (2 cm) elastic and buckle for the belt (page 98).

How to Cut a Poncho

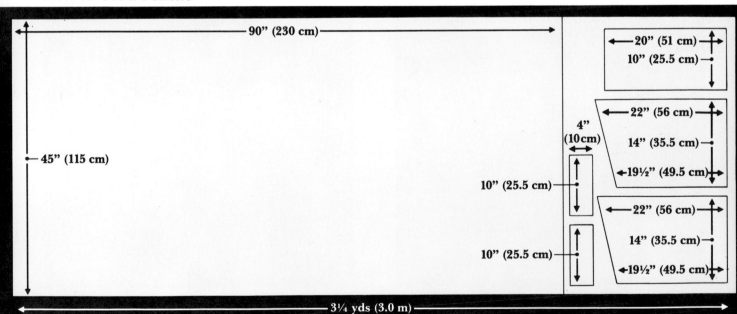

45" (115 cm) wide fabric. Straighten crosswise edges of fabric. Use ruler to draw cutting lines for one pocket, two collars, and two pocket flaps, as shown. For 45" by 90" (115 by 230 cm) poncho section, use full width of fabric. Selvages provide two prefinished edges for poncho; finish two raw edges with narrow

topstitched hem. For 60" (150 cm) wide fabric, draw cutting lines for pocket, collars, and flaps along one lengthwise edge. For 45" by 90" (115 by 230 cm) poncho section, use full length of fabric; finish all edges with narrow topstitched hem.

How to Sew a Self-storing Poncho

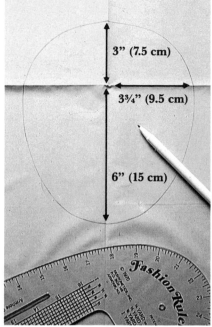

1) Fold poncho section in half crosswise, and finger press the crease. Fold poncho in half again, lengthwise. Draw cutting line for neckline as shown above; mark center back and center front. Cut out neckline.

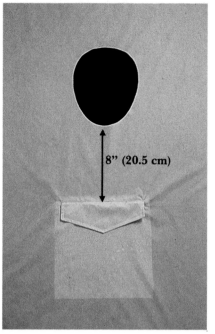

2) Stitch pocket and flap as for garment-storing pocket (pages 98 and 99). Place pocket 8" (20.5 cm) below center front mark.

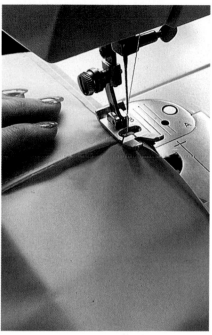

3) Stitch hood together matching long and short edges. Use narrow French seams, or serge. Finish straight open end of hood with narrow topstitched hem.

4) Pin slanted open end of hood to poncho, right sides together, with long seam of hood at center front. Stitch ¼" (6 mm) seam and zigzag raw edges together.

5) Fold poncho on shoulder crease with wrong sides together. Use closely spaced zigzag stitches to make a bar tack 18" (46 cm) from fold to form armhole on each side.

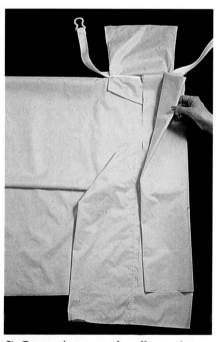

6) Open zipper and pull out the pocket. Lay poncho out flat, and fold at pocket line. Fold sides toward center. Push fabric at pocket opening into pocket. Fold the poncho into the pocket, and close the zipper.

Sewing Polar Fleece

Polar fleece is a popular outerwear fabric because it provides warmth without bulk or weight, is machine washable, and is easy to sew. Polar fleece will not ravel, so the raw edges of seams do not require finishing. Because polar fleece has a brushed surface texture, use a "with nap" pattern layout so the color looks uniform in the finished garment.

Although polar fleece can be used for warm unlined jackets, tops, and pull-on pants, it is not waterproof or windproof. For the best protection from the weather, wear a windproof or water repellent shell over a polar fleece garment. Or use polar fleece as a lining for a jacket, vest, or raincoat.

To minimize pilling, turn garments inside out when washing them. Pilling does not affect the insulating quality of polar fleece.

Finish edges of polar fleece garments with ribbing, serging, or contrasting binding. Cut binding from nylon/spandex two-way stretch knit to create an attractive contrast in texture. Stretch the knit binding as you sew it to the garment and the edge stretches like an elasticized binding. Hems, casings, and other self-fabric finishes are too bulky.

Serging techniques work well on polar fleece and shorten sewing time by automatically trimming seam allowances to reduce bulk. The slightly wider seam sewn by a four-thread serger is practical for the thickness of polar fleece, although the narrower seam sewn by a three-thread serger is also acceptable. On a conventional sewing machine, simply straight-stitch seams. To reduce bulk, trim seam allowances to ¼" (6 mm) after sewing. The raw edges will not ravel.

How to Bind an Edge with Two-way Stretch Knit

1) Trim hem or seam allowance off garment edge. Cut 2" (5 cm) wide binding crosswise from nylon/spandex two-way stretch knit, equal to three-fourths the measurement of garment edge.

2) Stitch short ends of binding together in ¼" (6 mm) seam, right sides together. If binding waistline of zip-front jacket, omit this seam. Fold binding in half lengthwise. Divide garment edge and binding into fourths, and mark with pins.

3) Pin binding to right side of garment, with raw edges even and pin markers matching. Stitch ¼" (6 mm) seam, using long straight stitch and stretching binding to fit edge as you sew.

4) Fold binding over stitching to wrong side of garment. From right side, edgestitch binding along fold, stretching binding as you sew.

5) Finished bound edges on polar fleece sleeves and hem stretch like an elasticized binding.

Insulated Outerwear

The triple layers of an insulated garment require different fabrics for the outer shell, the insulation, and the lining. The outer shell receives the most wear and is exposed to the weather. Use a tightly woven, durable fabric that offers protection from wind and water, such as coated or uncoated nylon ripstop or nylon taffeta; tri-blend, a mixture of three fibers, usually cotton, polyester, and nylon; or bi-blend, a mixture of two fibers, usually nylon combined with either cotton or polyester.

The insulation that keeps you warm is the middle fabric layer. Insulating fabrics available for sewing are described on pages 14 and 15.

The lining primarily hides raw edges and protects the insulation from abrasion. It should be lightweight to avoid adding bulk to the jacket. It should also be slick so it slides easily over other clothing. Care requirements of a lining should match those of the outer shell. Lightweight, slippery nylon is an ideal lining for jackets with nylon or nylon blend outer shells.

An insulated vest makes a good beginning project. After mastering the techniques for the vest, you will find an insulated jacket is not difficult to sew.

Layout and Cutting Techniques

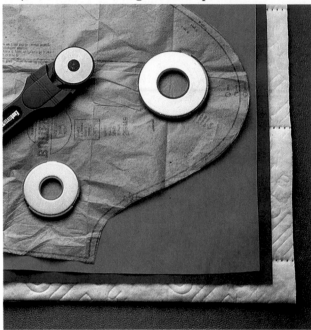

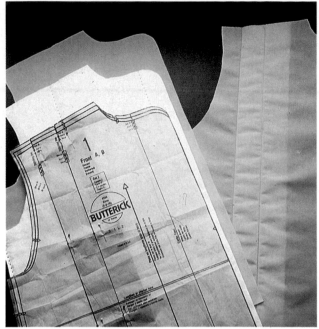

Stack lining, insulation, and shell fabric for layout and cutting. Use weights to hold the pattern in place. Cut all three layers at once with rotary cutter or sharp shears. Flip pattern pieces over to cut the right and left-hand sides.

Reduce bulk by folding details such as tucks, gathers, or pleats out of pattern to cut lining and insulation. Cut shell separately, using complete pattern. To prevent raveling, sear nylon fabrics immediately after cutting.

How to Handle Insulated Fabrics

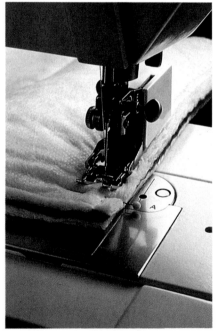

1) Machine-baste insulation sections to wrong side of shell sections ¼" (6 mm) from edges. Use Even Feed™ foot, or hold layers taut in front of and behind presser foot. Do not use serging or overcasting; the extra thread makes seam allowances unnecessarily bulky.

2) Handle insulation and outer shell fabrics as one layer. To stitch, pin right sides of shell together, and use Even Feed™ foot or taut sewing to prevent uneven feeding. Do not pull fabric under the needle. Use as many pins as necessary to hold in place.

3) Topstitch set-in sleeves, raglan sleeves, and shoulder seams. Finger press seam to one side; from right side, stitch close to seam. This reinforces and strengthens the seam. It may be necessary to trim corners and grade seams before topstitching.

Insulated Vests

The insulated vest has become a staple in many ski wardrobes because it offers warmth plus freedom of arm movement. A basic vest pattern can be used over and over with a different look each time. Contrasting lining, for example, is a simple way to create fashion interest. Applied stripes of contrasting fabric also add fashion appeal without making the project difficult to sew.

Because an insulated garment has separate fabric layers for the outer shell, the insulation, and the lining, in effect you must cut three separate

garments from the main pattern pieces. The methods used for sewing a vest eliminate all hand stitching, so the vest is turned to the right side through openings left in seams.

A front closure with snaps is an easy technique for a beginning project. If your pattern calls for a zipper, insert it after you assemble the shell and the lining but before you sew them together. Use the same techniques as for inserting a zipper in a basic jacket shell (pages 94 and 95).

1) Stitch shoulder seams of shell. Finger press to one side; on right side, stitch close to seam. Stitch shoulder seams of lining the same way. Stitch collar sections together; trim and clip seam, and turn right side out. Topstitch.

2) Slip lining into shell, right sides together and shoulder seams matching. Pin lining to shell at armholes. Stitch with 3-step zipzag; trim seam allowances to ¼" (6 mm).

3) Pin collar to shell with upper collar facing right side of lining. Pin lining and shell together at neckline and front edges.

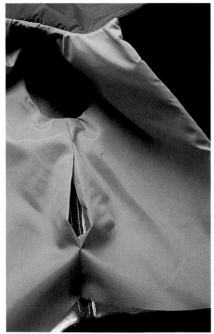

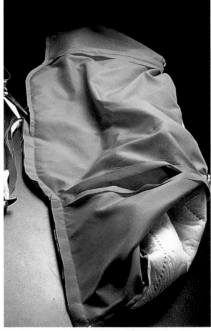

7) Stitch other side seam of vest and lining as in step 6, above, except leave 6" (15 cm) of lining side seam open. Opening is used later to turn vest right side out.

8) Turn vest inside out through lower edge. Pin vest to lining along lower edge, right sides together. Stitch seam; trim seam allowances. Trim diagonally across corners at bottom of front opening.

9) Turn vest right side out through opening in lining side seam, being careful not to rip seam.

4) Stitch shell and lining from center back of neckline to bottom of each front edge (arrows). Trim seam allowances to ¼" (6 mm). Clip neckline curve.

5) Turn vest right side out by pulling front section through shoulder area toward back of vest. Turn one side of vest at a time.

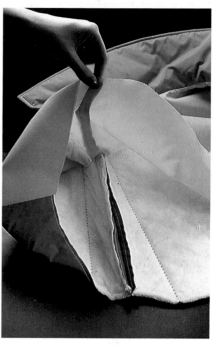

6) Pin vest front to vest back and lining front to lining back at one side seam, right sides together. Stitch one continuous side seam, starting at lower edge of vest and stopping at lower edge of lining.

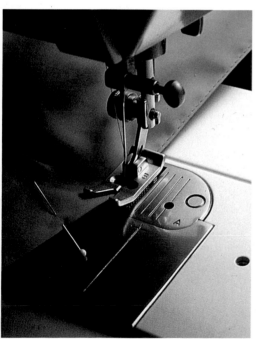

10) Fold seam allowances under at side seam opening. Pin folds together, and edgestitch folds to close opening in seam.

11) Topstitch around all edges of vest, including armholes.

12) Apply gripper snaps for front closing, using two snaps on collar. To protect work surface, place small block of wood under fabric when attaching snaps.

Insulated Jackets

An insulated jacket and a basic shell use many of the same sewing techniques. Attaching the lining and handling the bulk of the insulation make the jacket more time-consuming to sew, but the results are well worth the effort.

Cut the upper collar from the shell fabric and insulation, and the undercollar from lining fabric to reduce bulk. Cut in-seam pockets from the shell fabric only, because the jacket lining will cover the raw edges.

Check the sleeve length during the try-on fitting of the lining. This is the most common fitting adjustment required. If the sleeves will be finished with ribbing cuffs, fit the sleeves to the first knuckle of the thumb for wearing ease. If the jacket is for a growing child, fit the sleeves to the first knuckle of the index finger for extra length.

How to Prepare the Jacket and Lining

1) Construct jacket lining; to reinforce seams, press to one side and topstitch close to seamline. Stitch jacket upper collar to lining. Try.on the lining to check the fit. This is the easiest time to make any necessary changes.

2) Add stripes or piping (pages 116 to 121) to outer fabric. Machine-baste shell and insulation sections together (page 108).

3) Insert zippered pockets (pages 96 and 97) before joining jacket sections. Stitching on flat sections is easier than on shaped garment.

4) Stitch jacket shoulder and sleeve seams. Edgestitch seams for additional strength. Stitch underarm and side seams.

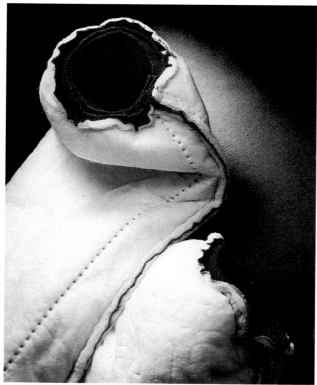

5) Attach ribbed cuffs (page 69). After stitching in place, do not turn them out. They should be in this position to attach lining.

6) Attach undercollar to jacket. Stitch one side of waistband to lower edge (page 93). Insert zipper (pages 94 and 95, steps 1 to 5). Final stitching on zipper is done after lining is attached.

How to Line an Insulated Jacket

1) Match shell and lining sleeve seams, being careful not to twist lining sleeves. Pin lining to shell, turning back raw edge of lining to match edge of cuff. Right side of lining is facing cuff; cuff is between shell and lining.

2) Stitch around each sleeve opening on top of cuff seam stitching. The lining is not inside the jacket for this stitching.

3) Finished cuff seam has lining attached to shell with cuff sandwiched between. This method provides a sturdy machine finish and eliminates hand stitching.

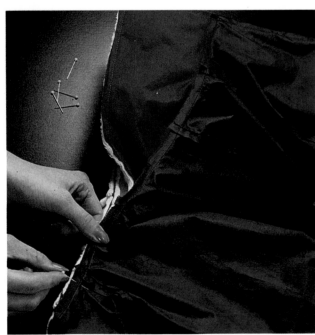

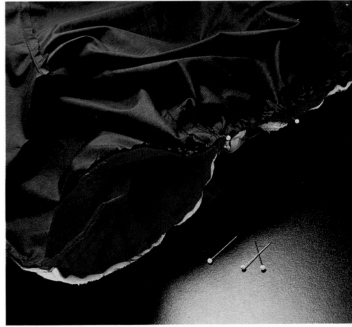

7) Push collar down between shell and lining to pin neckline seam allowances together, matching center back of shell neckline to center back of lining. Stitch seam allowances together, beginning slightly before one shoulder seam and stitching slightly beyond other shoulder seam. Stitching helps collar roll properly and tacks lining permanently to shell.

8) Push waistband up between shell and lining to pin waistband seam allowances together, matching center back of shell to center back of lining. Stitch seam allowances together to tack shell permanently to lining, stretching as you sew. Begin and end stitching near zipper at front closing.

4) Turn outer shell and lining wrong side out. Position shell and lining with right sides together. Pin free edge of waistband ribbing to lining, right sides together. Stitch in ¼" (6 mm) seam, stretching ribbing to fit as you sew.

5) Pin upper collar of lining and undercollar of shell together with right sides facing. Pin lining to front edges of shell, folding waistband up and zipper teeth in toward right side of shell.

6) Stitch front edges and outer edge of collar to lining; leave 8" (20.5 cm) of seam unstitched at the center of one front edge to provide opening for turning jacket right side out. Backstitch to reinforce ends of opening.

9) Turn jacket right side out through opening at front zipper closing. Pull small portions of jacket through opening, working slowly to avoid tearing fabric at top and bottom of opening.

10) Turn seam allowance of lining under at front opening. Use glue stick, pins, or hand basting to attach folded seam allowance to zipper tape.

11) Topstitch collar and front of jacket ¼" to ⅜" (6 mm to 1 cm) from zipper seam and collar edges. Topstitching keeps lining neatly in place and prevents it from becoming caught in zipper closure.

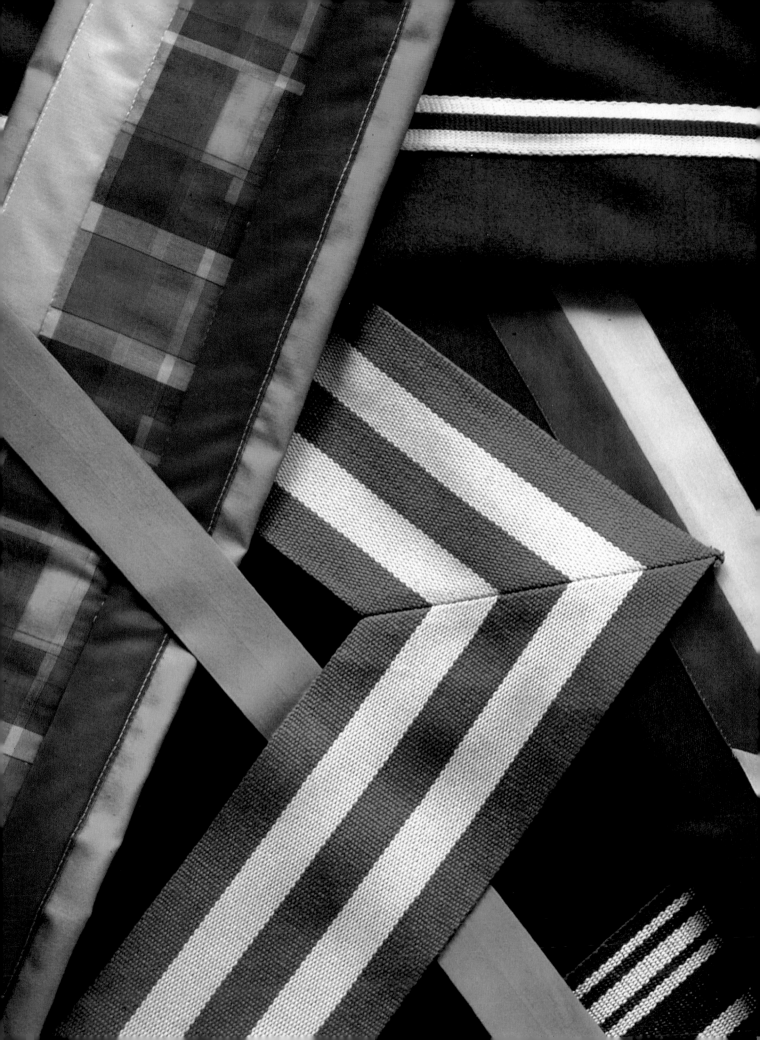

Applied Stripes

Applied stripes are made by topstitching one or more strips of fabric onto garment sections. They offer an easy way to achieve the look of fine detailing on fashion sportswear. Creative variations of applied stripes all use similar, basic sewing techniques.

The simplest form of applied stripe is a single strip of contrasting fabric. The strip may be as wide or narrow as desired. Use a single strip on the front of a garment, or position it on all garment sections so the stripe encircles the garment. For a custom touch, use the same fabric for small sections, such as undercollar and front facings.

You can also combine strips of various fabric prints and textures. Knits can be mixed with wovens, and mesh can be layered over smooth fabric textures. For an effective contrast in texture on knit garments use the wrong side of the fabric for applied stripes. Give applied stripes a soft, raised dimension by padding them with polyester batting.

Another way to add fashion interest is to use lightweight trims, such as ribbons, knitted braids, or flat piping, along the edges of fabric stripes. Braids and ribbons can also be used instead of fabric strips to make stripes.

An important guideline for applied stripes is to combine compatible fabric weights. The applied stripe should match the weight of the garment fabric or be lighter in weight. Also, use fabrics that have the same care requirements. If combining dark or bright fabric colors with white or light fabric colors, be sure the dyes are colorfast so the dark or bright colors will not bleed or stain the lighter colors. Preshrink all fabrics before you cut.

How to Add an Applied Stripe

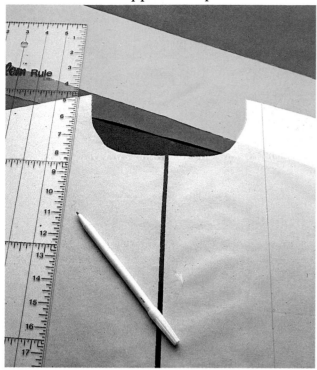

1) Mark placement guide for stripe ¼" (6 mm) inside the finished edge of stripe. Use liquid marking pen, or press a crease across garment section to indicate placement of stripe.

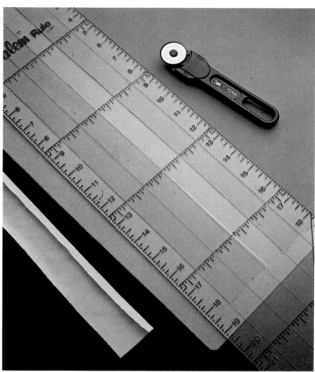

2) Cut out strip of desired width on straight fabric grain, allowing ¼" (6 mm) seam allowance on each long raw edge. Use transparent ruler and rotary cutter for quick, accurate cutting. Fold under one long raw edge ¼" (6 mm), and press.

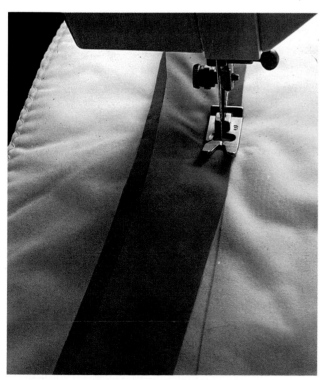

3) Place strip so unfolded raw edge lines up with marked placement guide. Right side of strip and garment section are facing. Stitch strip to garment ¼" (6 mm) from raw edge of strip.

4) Fold strip over stitching so it is right side up. Press; pin. Edgestitch fold. Edgestitch opposite side of strip in same direction to prevent shifting.

How to Apply a Narrow Stripe

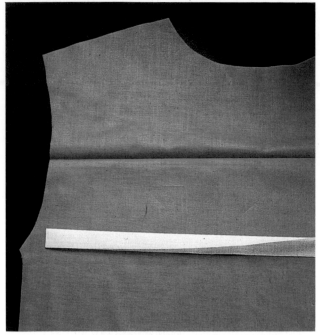

1) Cut strip as in step 2, page 117, but cut it double width. Fold strip along its length, wrong sides together, and press. Mark placement guide as in step 1, page 117.

2) Stitch one side of strip to garment as in step 3, page 117. Fold strip over raw edges, press, and edgestitch. Edgestitch opposite side of strip in same direction. Since this side is prefinished, it is not necessary to turn under the edge.

How to Apply a Braid Stripe

1) Preshrink braid; steam it thoroughly because knitted trims can shrink considerably. Hold steam iron slightly above surface of braid.

2) Mark placement guide for braid on garment section; pressing a crease is fastest marking method. Align one edge of braid with marking. Position braid with dissolvable basting tape. Stitch with conventional foot; or pin and edgestitch, using Even Feed™ foot. Edgestitch both sides of braid in same direction.

Applying Multiple Stripes

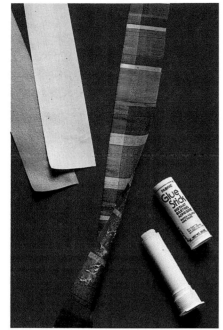

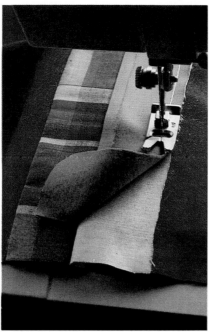

Lapped method. 1) Apply first fabric strip using basic method, page 117, but omit pressing under one raw edge and final edgestitching. Use glue stick to baste raw edge of strip to garment.

2) Stitch second strip over first, using raw edge as placement guide. Stitch succeeding strips same way, turning under raw edge of final strip for edgestitching. Lapped method makes lightweight fabrics and narrow stripes easier to handle.

Pieced method. Join all fabric strips, using ¼" (6 mm) seam allowances. Press seams toward one side, pressing all seams in same direction. Apply strip using basic method, page 117, treating the pieced strip as one strip of fabric.

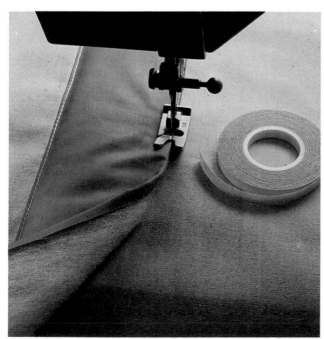

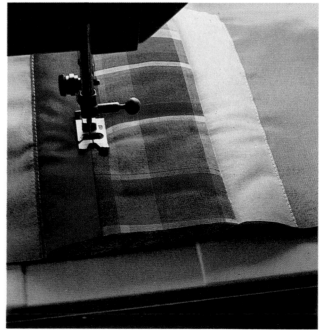

Padded stripes. Use basic method, page 117, but insert strip of polyester batting under fabric strip before edgestitching second side. Batting is cut to match finished size of applied stripe. Baste batting in place with glue stick or basting tape if necessary.

Multiple padded stripes. Stitch fabric strips together using pieced method, above. Cut polyester batting to match finished size of multiple stripe. Apply multiple stripe to garment, using basic method on page 117 and inserting batting before final edgestitching. Topstitch through all layers, stitching on top of seams that join individual strips.

Piping

Piping is a narrow, folded strip of fabric that is inserted in a garment seam. Effective places for this tailored trim include collars, pocket openings, pants and shorts side seams, and the slanted seams of raglan sleeves. Besides looking attractive, piping also stabilizes seams and makes them stronger. Piped seams should not be used on stretch knit garments that are closely fitted.

Piping is an easy trim to make. Cut a fabric strip 1⅝" (4 cm) wide to make piping filled with four-ply acrylic yarn. If using woven fabric, cut the strip on the true bias grain. Find the true bias by folding the fabric diagonally so the selvage lines up with the crosswise edge. Mark the cutting lines parallel to the fold. If using knitted fabric, cut so the greater fabric stretch runs along the length of the strip.

How to Make Piping with Yarn Filler

1) **Center** yarn on wrong side of bias strip. Fold strip over yarn, matching raw edges of strip.

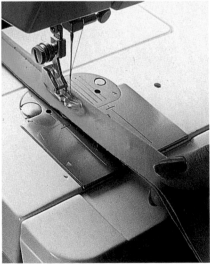

2) **Machine-baste** close to yarn, using zipper foot. To remove fabric slack and create smooth piping, stretch strip slightly as you sew. Trim seam allowance of piping to match seam allowance of garment.

Optional step. Remove yarn after application. This creates a flat piping that stretches slightly, a plus for knit garments such as T-shirts, sweatshirts, and sweatpants.

How to Make Flat Piping from Purchased Bias Tape

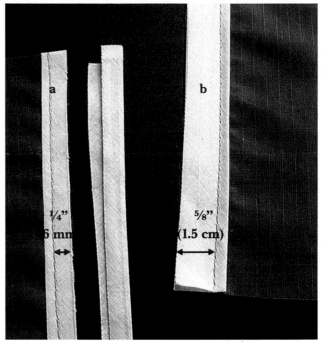

1) Press open 1" (2.5 cm) wide single-fold bias tape, eliminating folded-under edges. Fold tape in half, wrong sides together, and press. Because fabric slack has already been removed from purchased bias tape, do not stretch tape as you press.

2) Mark tape a distance from fold equal to finished width of piping plus seam allowance. Trim on marked line (**a**). For ⅛" (3 mm) wide piping with ⅝" (1.5 cm) seam allowance, no trimming is needed (**b**). Precut tape, when folded in half, is ready to apply.

How to Insert Piping in a Seam

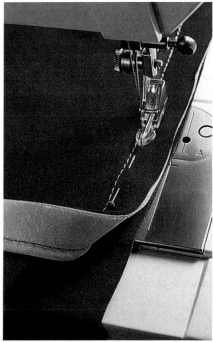

1) Pin piping to right side of garment section, matching raw edges of piping to raw edge of seam allowance. Machine-baste piping to seamline. If applying yarn-filled piping, use zipper foot.

2) Curve ends of piping into seam allowance at inconspicuous place. At ends, pull bias back to uncover cord; remove cord or yarn filler to eliminate bulk in seam where ends cross.

3) Pin adjoining garment section over basted piping, right sides together. Stitch seam, sewing on top of machine basting.

Fold-over Braid

Fold-over braid is used to bind garment edges. It is especially suitable as a finishing technique for garments made from thick or bulky fabrics. Hems, seams, and facings can then be omitted, creating flatter and smoother edges.

Fold-over braid comes in folded and flat forms. Some braids are pressed so the edges do not meet. When applying the braid, place the wider side underneath the garment, and the narrower side on top. Flat fold-over braid has a raised thread or other folding guideline positioned slightly off-center throughout its length. When applying the braid, place the raw edge of the garment along this guideline, so the wider portion of the braid is underneath the garment. With some braids it is possible to stitch only once to secure both edges of the braid.

Considerable shrinkage can occur with these trims, so preshrinking is an important preliminary step. Preshrink by thorough steaming. Hold the iron just above the surface of the braid, and allow the steam to penetrate. Wait until the braid is cool and dry before handling it. To make braid easier to apply to curved edges such as necklines, preshape the braid to match curve, using the same steaming technique.

How to Apply Fold-over Braid

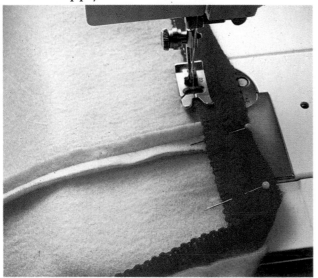

1) Open braid out flat. Pin braid to garment, wrong sides together, with fold of braid at cut edge. Stitch close to edge of braid.

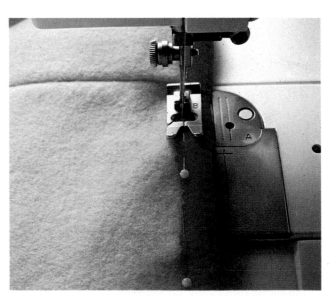

2) Fold braid over to right side, enclosing cut edge; edgestitch from right side.

How to Join Ends of Fold-over Braid

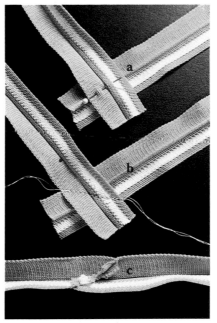

1) Mark seamline where ends of braid meet. Before cutting braid to proper length, add to each end a seam allowance equal to total width of braid.

2) Lap ends of braid at right angles, right sides together **(a)**. Stitch diagonally across ends **(b)**. Press seam open. Trim to ¼" (6 mm). Trim out V-shape to reduce bulk at foldline **(c)**.

3) Apply braid to garment as in steps 1 and 2, page 122. Position braid seam next to garment seam, rather than on top of seam to reduce bulk. When braid is folded into finished position, diagonal seam staggers bulky seam allowances for smooth edge.

How to Miter Corners of Fold-over Braid

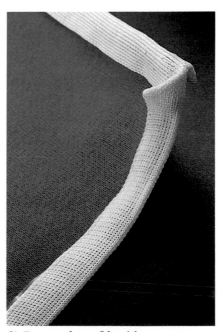

1) Baste edge of braid to right side of garment, using basting tape. At corner, fold braid back on itself, right sides together. Use pin to mark distance from corner equal to finished width of braid.

2) Fold braid diagonally at pin marker, bringing edge of braid into position along garment edge. Use basting tape to baste braid for short distance past corner.

3) Baste edge of braid on wrong side of garment around corner, making similar diagonal fold in braid. Aim miter in opposite direction from fold on right side of garment to reduce bulk.

Belts

Belts are easy to make at a cost far less than comparable ready-made styles. Use a strip of self-fabric for a belt, or purchase belting by the yard (meter). Stretch or woven belting requires no interfacing, stiffener, or lining, and most beltings have prefinished long edges. As a result, making a belt can be as simple as trimming belting to the right length and attaching a buckle.

A crush belt that wraps around the waist is softer and less tailored than classic belts made from crisp beltings. Use a crush belt to dress up simple sportswear ensembles or add interest to pullover tunics and dresses. This belt takes minutes to make. Use wide woven belting; instead of a buckle, use hook and loop tape for a closure.

For a belt that requires a buckle, choose from a clamp, double bar, single bar, or D-buckle.

Clamp buckle requires no sewing. Slip the end of the belting into the clamp, then close the clamp. The teeth grip the belting securely.

Double bar buckle is another no-sew buckle. Slip the end of the belting over the first bar and under the second. Changing from one belting to another is easy with this style of buckle.

Single bar buckle requires stitching to secure the end of the belting. Finish the raw edge of the belting with liquid fray preventer or closely spaced zigzag stitches.

D-buckles are made of plastic or metal and sold in pairs. They also require stitching to secure the ends.

Finishing Techniques for the End of a Belt

Mitering. Fold belting in half along its length, with right sides together. Stitch ¼" (6 mm) seam **(a)**. Finger press seam open; then turn right side out **(b)**. Point feeds easily through belt buckle.

Fringing. Mark woven belting to indicate desired length of fringe. Straight-stitch over marking. Use pin to remove threads from raw edge of belting up to stitching.

Stitching. Trim to straighten end. Apply liquid fray preventer on cut edge. Turn under ⅜" (1 cm), tucking under corners at an angle **(a)**. Insert buckle. Stitch ¼" (6 mm) from fold, backstitching at start and finish to secure stitching **(b)**.

How to Make a Crush Belt

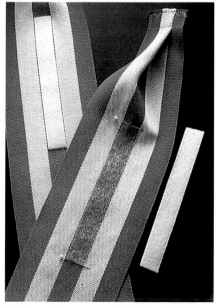

1) Cut 3" to 4" (7.5 to 10 cm) wide webbing 12" (30.5 cm) longer than waist measurement. Cut two strips of hook tape as long as half the webbing width; cut two strips of loop tape 6" (15 cm) long. Cut two strips of fusible web 6" (15 cm) long and as wide as tape.

2) Pin pleat in each end of the webbing, making pleats deep enough to reduce webbing to half original width. Zigzag or serge to finish raw edges. Stitch one strip of hook tape on right side of each end, stitching through pleats.

3) Fuse loop tape 5" (12.5 cm) from each end on wrong side. Layer web under tape, centering tape on belt. Fuse from right side. To wear belt, wrap around waist and tuck ends under; use hook and loop tape to hold ends in place.

Index

Cy DeCosse Incorporated offers
fine sewing accessories to subscribers.
For information write:

Sewing Accessories
5900 Green Oak Drive
Minnetonka, MN 55343